Clinical Psychology: A Very Short Introduction

VERY SHORT INTRODUCTIONS are for anyone wanting a stimulating and accessible way into a new subject. They are written by experts, and have been translated into more than 45 different languages.

The series began in 1995, and now covers a wide variety of topics in every discipline. The VSI library now contains over 500 volumes—a Very Short Introduction to everything from Psychology and Philosophy of Science to American History and Relativity—and continues to grow in every subject area.

Very Short Introductions available now:

ACCOUNTING Christopher Nobes
ADOLESCENCE Peter K. Smith
ADVERTISING Winston Fletcher
AFRICAN AMERICAN RELIGION
 Eddie S. Glaude Jr
AFRICAN HISTORY John Parker and
 Richard Rathbone
AFRICAN RELIGIONS Jacob K. Olupona
AGEING Nancy A. Pachana
AGNOSTICISM Robin Le Poidevin
AGRICULTURE Paul Brassley and
 Richard Soffe
ALEXANDER THE GREAT
 Hugh Bowden
ALGEBRA Peter M. Higgins
AMERICAN HISTORY Paul S. Boyer
AMERICAN IMMIGRATION
 David A. Gerber
AMERICAN LEGAL HISTORY
 G. Edward White
AMERICAN POLITICAL HISTORY
 Donald Critchlow
AMERICAN POLITICAL PARTIES
 AND ELECTIONS L. Sandy Maisel
AMERICAN POLITICS
 Richard M. Valelly
THE AMERICAN PRESIDENCY
 Charles O. Jones
THE AMERICAN REVOLUTION
 Robert J. Allison
AMERICAN SLAVERY
 Heather Andrea Williams
THE AMERICAN WEST Stephen Aron
AMERICAN WOMEN'S HISTORY
 Susan Ware

ANAESTHESIA Aidan O'Donnell
ANARCHISM Colin Ward
ANCIENT ASSYRIA Karen Radner
ANCIENT EGYPT Ian Shaw
ANCIENT EGYPTIAN ART AND
 ARCHITECTURE Christina Riggs
ANCIENT GREECE Paul Cartledge
THE ANCIENT NEAR EAST
 Amanda H. Podany
ANCIENT PHILOSOPHY Julia Annas
ANCIENT WARFARE Harry Sidebottom
ANGELS David Albert Jones
ANGLICANISM Mark Chapman
THE ANGLO-SAXON AGE John Blair
ANIMAL BEHAVIOUR
 Tristram D. Wyatt
THE ANIMAL KINGDOM
 Peter Holland
ANIMAL RIGHTS David DeGrazia
THE ANTARCTIC Klaus Dodds
ANTISEMITISM Steven Beller
ANXIETY Daniel Freeman and
 Jason Freeman
THE APOCRYPHAL GOSPELS
 Paul Foster
ARCHAEOLOGY Paul Bahn
ARCHITECTURE Andrew Ballantyne
ARISTOCRACY William Doyle
ARISTOTLE Jonathan Barnes
ART HISTORY Dana Arnold
ART THEORY Cynthia Freeland
ASIAN AMERICAN HISTORY
 Madeline Y. Hsu
ASTROBIOLOGY David C. Catling
ASTROPHYSICS James Binney

Available soon:

For more information visit our website

www.oup.com/vsi/

Susan Llewelyn and Katie Aafjes-van Doorn

CLINICAL PSYCHOLOGY

A Very Short Introduction

OXFORD
UNIVERSITY PRESS

OXFORD
UNIVERSITY PRESS

Great Clarendon Street, Oxford, OX2 6DP,
United Kingdom

Oxford University Press is a department of the University of Oxford.
It furthers the University's objective of excellence in research, scholarship,
and education by publishing worldwide. Oxford is a registered trade mark of
Oxford University Press in the UK and in certain other countries

© Susan Llewelyn and Katie Aafjes-van Doorn 2017

The moral rights of the authors have been asserted

First edition published in 2017

Impression: 1

Published in the United States of America by Oxford University Press
198 Madison Avenue, New York, NY 10016, United States of America

British Library Cataloguing in Publication Data
Data available

Library of Congress Control Number: 2016957140

ISBN 978-0-19-875389-6

Printed in Great Britain by
Ashford Colour Press Ltd, Gosport, Hampshire

Contents

Acknowledgements

Helen Beinart, Guy Fielding, Josie Fielding, David Murphy, Bernard Kat, Agnès Couvée, Ton van Doorn.

Preface

What is clinical psychology?

If you were to meet either of us socially and enquire as to what we do for a living, you might be forgiven for thinking that our reply is rather vague. When people ask, we tend to answer with something like: 'A psychologist working in healthcare...', or, if pushed: 'We offer talking therapy to people who struggle with certain aspects of their lives...'. This is because explaining clinical psychology isn't simple: we do a wide range of things (including assessment, therapy, research, teaching, management, academic and clinical supervision) depending on where we work (from private practice to hospital, care home, prison, mental health clinic and in academia). Also, some people still find the subject a little alarming, imagining that we somehow know things by magic, or can read people's minds (which we most certainly can't!).

This VSI gives us the chance to describe the work of a clinical psychologist, which is both intriguing and challenging, dealing as it does with people's thoughts and emotions, and often with their distressing experiences or personal difficulties. Rather than labelling these experiences as symptoms of an illness or an indication of madness, clinical psychologists are curious about why these symptoms occur, wanting to understand feelings, thoughts, or behaviours in their context. Our intention is to empower people to find a way to feel better, by learning to tolerate, accept, or manage their distress differently, or by changing how people see themselves and their situation.

The essence of clinical psychology is the creative application of what we know from psychological theory and research to the unique, personal experiences of individuals who are facing difficulties or challenges in their lives. Further, we make a point of involving the people whom we are trying to help in decision-making (an approach sometimes called 'person-centred'), working from their own way of understanding their difficulties, and taking into account their social, cultural, or economic circumstances.

There is no single universal or definitive way of being a healthy person, hence no psychological theory fits everywhere, and much work is still needed to make sure clinical psychology is practised in a way that is culturally sensitive and responsive to all the people it aims to help. Within the field, arguments abound over whether clinical psychology can or should claim always to rest upon scientifically verifiable principles or research. Other areas of disagreement include whether clinical psychologists, by using psychiatric language, diagnoses, and working in medicalized care systems, are colluding in medicalizing and mystifying what is actually normal human misery or the consequence of social inequality. This VSI covers some of these areas of agreement and debate, and describes future developments of our profession in this increasingly technological and international world.

An important word is needed here about terminology: despite holding different, non-medical assumptions about the causes of much physical/emotional distress, most clinical psychologists work in healthcare settings, where 'patients' present for 'treatment' to 'cure' their 'symptoms'. Although better than labelling distress as 'madness' or 'lunacy', there are several downsides to this medical terminology. For example, it may convey the message that those in need of help are passive recipients of the skill of the expert clinician (as someone who has appendicitis would be), and that what is wrong with the person is something inside their bodies or brains that can be 'fixed', primarily by pharmaceutical or surgical means (as might be the case if they have malaria or a brain tumour).

For those reasons, some clinical psychologists prefer the use of the word 'client' instead of 'patient'. Others prefer to use the words 'experiences' rather than 'symptoms', thereby highlighting the potentially emotional, non-pathological nature of distress. This VSI mostly uses the word 'client' to reflect the emphasis on the active nature of the person receiving help, but on occasions, and especially when the person is receiving psychological input in association with medical care for physical health conditions (e.g. a stroke, cancer, or diabetes), the medically related terminology will be used. This is largely a matter of context, and does not imply an underlying difference in how the person is understood by the clinical psychologist.

Because clinical psychology is all about people, this VSI includes a variety of case studies and short accounts about the lives of real people. But as you can imagine, it is important not to betray the confidences of those who have shared parts of their lives with us. So all the stories included here have been altered slightly to preserve anonymity, and all names, places, or key identifying features have been similarly modified. Nevertheless, all the accounts are based on real people's psychological experiences, and will hopefully give you a flavour of the work done in our profession.

There are already some excellent VSIs in related areas, so we should explain what this one will add. VSIs have been written about specific client groups (e.g. on child psychology), or type of problems (e.g. autism or schizophrenia), or settings (e.g. forensic psychology), or theories (e.g. psychoanalysis). Yet other VSIs touch on clinical psychology briefly, as a sub-category of the wider field (e.g. the VSI on psychology). This VSI focuses solely on clinical psychology as a profession, showing how clinical psychologists might work with a particular set of people or problems in practice. Just like all other VSIs, this is not intended as a self-help book, but rather aims to give you an idea about the context in which you might encounter a clinical psychologist, their training and skills, and how they might go about their day-to-day activities.

List of illustrations

Chapter 1
Clinical psychologists at work

Most of us, if asked what we want in life, simply say we want to be happy and healthy. Children also say they want to feel safe in their families, to go to school, and to have friends. Most adults then add a number of fairly ordinary things, like productive work to do, maybe a long-term partner and a family, somewhere to live, and enough money. Yet for many of us, it often proves extraordinarily difficult to achieve these apparently simple aspects of life: tragedies strike, illnesses develop, intimate or family relationships break down, disappointments happen, and circumstances change. Being a happy, productive person isn't easy, especially in the face of ill health, trauma, loss, and unexpected challenges at work or home, abuse, isolation, or chronically difficult economic circumstances.

Clinical psychologists are people who aim to offer psychological help to those who are unhappy or struggling with certain aspects of their lives; and to those who are ill, especially when their mental health is adversely affected. Many of their clients experience uncomfortable feelings (see Figure 1), such as anxiety, loneliness, or rejection, or may sometimes find personal relationships difficult. Some clinical psychologists also work with those who want to learn more about themselves and to understand their emotions better. Others work with organizations who want to use a psychological perspective to help their workforce. Clinical psychologists' training is based on an in-depth understanding of the human psyche,

1. People experience a wide range of sometimes uncomfortable feelings.

focusing on the development and maintenance of emotional and cognitive health, with the aim of reducing distress and promoting mental health. This VSI will describe people who have consulted clinical psychologists and whose experiences include a wide range of difficulties, thereby illustrating the work that we do (see Box 1).

Numbers of people needing the help of clinical psychologists

Estimates vary about the number of those who might benefit. For centuries people have taken their problems to socially sanctioned

Box 1 Examples of people described in this VSI who seek help from clinical psychologists

Polly is a 13-year-old girl who has started drastically controlling what she eats and is losing so much weight that her family are getting worried. Steve's life has progressively collapsed; his mental health deteriorated after he became unemployed and now he faces repeated admissions for psychiatric care. Roger and his wife are contemplating a miserable future following his stroke and the subsequent deterioration of their relationship. Cassie is a 15-year-old who has been harming herself; while Ryan and Judy are despairing about their relationship with their 5-year-old adopted son, Tom. Meanwhile Sara is helping her team to work more effectively with abused children; and Nicky wants to improve her personal relationships.

healers including faith healers, fortune tellers, clergy, and medical doctors. Clinical psychologists are a relatively new and scarce resource; hence many people don't have access to psychological expertise, even though they might benefit from it. Estimates suggest that three-quarters of people who have a treatable mental health problem currently receive little or no treatment; and more than half of the people who go to see their family doctor have either primary or concurrent mental health difficulties. Most people with physical conditions such as cancer, diabetes, or heart disease are also likely to experience some degree of anxiety or depression. At least one in three people are likely to be experiencing some level of emotional distress at any one time, and the chances of having some form of mental health problem during a person's lifetime is about 50 per cent. Yet mental health is not given the same emphasis as physical health, meaning that much less money is spent on treating mental than physical health, and much smaller sums are devoted to researching psychological than physical conditions.

Besides failing to reduce immediate emotional suffering, this has huge implications for people's long-term health outcomes. For example, those with the most severe mental health problems are likely to die around fifteen to twenty years earlier than others without these problems. Young people are also poorly served: studies in the UK, for example, suggest that around 10 per cent of those aged between 5 and 16 have mental health problems, but very few have good access to services. Inevitably this leads to longer term, probably preventable, distress. This is unfortunate. Half of those with long-term mental health conditions first experienced symptoms in their early to mid-teens; yet we often fail to identify or treat these conditions. Things are no better at the other end of the lifespan: only quite recently have the psychological needs of the elderly been recognized, and there is a worrying lack of services geared specifically for them.

The contribution of clinical psychology

If someone is distressed, it is of course important to check out what is going on and why. Many of life's problems don't need a clinical psychologist, and can be resolved with practical help from a lawyer, doctor, financial advisor, or teacher, or simply by accessing more resources such as money, goods, or access to education or information. But a psychologist can help to explore the unhelpful, confusing, or self-defeating things that we sometimes do, think, or feel. The essence of the clinical psychologist's work is a collaborative examination of what seems to be causing us emotional distress, and an active exploration of ways of tolerating, understanding, or alleviating this. The help offered is based on the clinical psychologist's understanding of how human beings ordinarily develop and function, and what happens when people get stuck.

How clinical psychologists train, think, and understand people

All clinical psychologists are required to have an undergraduate qualification in academic psychology, which acts as the foundation for their clinical work (just like medical doctors are required to have a basic education in anatomy, physiology, biochemistry, and genetics, before learning how to diagnose and treat physical illnesses).

Although there is no universally agreed undergraduate curriculum, a psychology degree normally focuses on a number of core topics about human functioning. These include learning and memory (how we process and store information); cognition (how we think and reason); communication (how we develop and use language); motivation and emotion (how we feel); perception (how we interpret and understand the world around us); social behaviour (how we interact with others and in groups); biology, physiology, and the brain (how the body influences us); development (how we change from birth to death); and personality (how we differ from one another). All of these topics will underpin the clinical psychologist's work in practice.

Undergraduate education also teaches students how to think about people, and how to find out more. Probably the predominant model in much contemporary psychology is that of the human as a living, embodied 'information processor'. In this model, humans are conceptualized as biological units who perceive, learn, interpret, process, act upon, modify, communicate, and produce meanings, albeit in a social context which strongly influences and shapes the process. By using scientific methods and ideas, clinical psychologists try to observe and understand humans with health concerns by developing theories and hypotheses about how and why people act or think as they do, and then to test out those hypotheses through observation or experimentation. Empirical, observable facts are considered much more useful than speculation or argument.

Most people nowadays agree that psychology is a science (even if it is an imperfect one) and that trying to conduct research objectively is the best way to gain a reasonably robust understanding of how people tick, and how to help them. There are however many debates about how scientific psychology really is, including its scope and validity. These debates include the criticism that humans are essentially unable to act as scientists about themselves; that the measures used are inevitably inadequate; that research is over-reliant on quantitative measures; that what is essentially human is not amenable to scientific observations or measurement; and that psychology focuses too much on the individual person even though many of the forces that shape our behaviour in fact lie elsewhere, either in wider society or in our genetic make-up and biology.

Although the part of the undergraduate psychology curriculum that deals most directly with emotional distress and mental health is sometimes labelled 'abnormal psychology', in fact the experience of emotional distress is really common. Much of the distress that is classified as 'abnormal' actually comprises behaviour or emotion that is understandable, and that results from comprehensible psychological processes, even if these sometimes work out poorly for the individual or for those around them. For example, an elderly man suddenly refusing to leave home for no apparent reason may be classified as behaving 'abnormally'. This behaviour might, however, be quite understandable if we take account of his anxiety about getting lost because of his failing eyesight and memory difficulties (which he has not told anybody about due both to a sense of shame and his reduced cognitive awareness). Likewise, feeling anxious about how other people judge us is pretty universal, although social anxiety is sometimes labelled in textbooks as an 'abnormality'.

Clinical psychologists argue that much behaviour considered in textbooks, and by society as a whole, as abnormal (such as being anxious, hearing voices in the absence of others, experiencing hallucinations, or feeling depressed despite apparently possessing many of the good things in life) is in fact understandable, if only the context and history of that behaviour or emotion were to be fully explored. Clinical psychologists also point out how we frequently try to cope with difficulties by using strategies that have been helpful or even necessary to us in the past, but might no longer be the most adaptive or helpful way of coping with a problem in the present.

Take, for example, a student who in the past had successfully hidden her severe anxiety about being assessed. Despite having a new and sympathetic teacher, our student might conceal exactly how far behind she is in completing an assignment. This protects her from risking an uncomfortable discussion in the short term, but it also prevents her from doing anything constructive to resolve her longer term difficulties. Working from this viewpoint, clinical psychologists don't blame people for their difficulties or unhelpful patterns of coping, but aim to work collaboratively to understand and resolve distress so that people can handle life's challenges better in the future.

Where clinical psychology came from and when: a very brief history

Clinical psychology as a way of addressing emotional distress has grown astonishingly quickly, and is still growing. People no longer immediately assume that you need to be mentally ill or mad to require the help of a clinical psychologist. Happily, increased public acceptance of the usefulness of gaining psychological understanding of emotional problems has opened up a range of options for a variety of conditions that were previously simply medicated, silenced, or just swept under the carpet of social indifference and embarrassment. Overall, in recent years, the stigma of consulting a clinical psychologist has significantly reduced.

Clinical psychology is a young profession, like its parent discipline of academic psychology, which only emerged properly in the latter part of the 19th century. The earliest reference to a 'clinical psychologist' was in 1896, while the first systematic applications of what we now think of as the principles of clinical psychology took place in the early 1920s.

This was work with troubled children, and also with members of the armed forces discharged after the end of World War I. Following this, clinical psychologists began contributing to the assessment and categorization of people who at that time were being housed in large mental institutions. At this point, psychologists were really just acting as scientific assistants to the medically trained psychiatrists who were in charge of the inmates. Originally this work was done largely to benefit institutions by sorting out and allocating labels to people thought to be mentally ill or 'retarded'. But by the middle of the 20th century, clinical psychologists began to contribute more significantly as clinicians in their own right, mainly by conducting more thorough assessments.

Over the next few decades, clinical psychologists working in mental hospitals then started to explore the possibilities of providing treatment through applying the principles of behaviour modification. This led to the development of behaviour therapy for a range of psychological difficulties (see Chapter 3 for more discussion of what these approaches entail). Achievements in understanding and assessing the brain also led to developments in applied neuropsychology, allowing clinical psychologists to contribute to the assessment and rehabilitation of those with brain injuries or brain damage.

The development of cognitive psychology from the 1960s onwards had a hugely beneficial impact on clinical psychology, inspiring the use of psychological models to understand and treat a wide range of conditions and problems. By the last quarter of the 20th century, clinical psychologists were participating fully in mental healthcare across the lifespan, using a variety of psychological interventions based on a wide range of theories and therapies. Clinical psychologists now work as fully independent professionals in many settings, and provide therapies for numerous mental health difficulties, based soundly on evidence from psychological research, They also have a significant role as researchers and clinical leaders of mental health services.

How clinical psychology is different

The essence of the clinical psychologist's work is making use of a core set of theories, methods, and competencies (see Chapters 2 and 3) in order to understand, assess, and provide help for people accessing mental healthcare: primarily, but not only, those with psychological distress. Unlike many others working in the field of mental health (see Box 2), most clinical psychologists

Box 2 How do clinical psychologists differ from other mental health practitioners?

Psychiatrists are specialist medical doctors who have a thorough understanding of physiology, anatomy, biochemistry, genetics, and pharmacology. After medical training, they chose to specialize in mental health. Broadly speaking, they use a medical model of mental illness—that is, they consider the presence of unusual or distressing thoughts, actions, and behaviours as symptoms of a biologically determined illness. Treatment normally includes medication or other physical interventions, together with careful personal management. After assessment, patients are typically seen in brief 10–20-minute follow-up sessions.

Psychotherapists and counsellors are people who aim to help others to understand themselves and their relationships better through talking. Some work with their clients by developing individually designed plans of treatment, focused on adapting to

(continued)

Box 2 Continued

situations, or changing problematic behaviour and experiences. Others use more open-ended approaches, aimed at increasing someone's self-knowledge. Medication is not prescribed, and less emphasis is usually placed on academic evidence and research. Psychotherapy and counselling normally involve the client and therapist developing a trusting professional relationship over weeks or months so that the client's problematic issues can be explored in a safe but highly personal context. These techniques may also be used by other professionals, including psychiatrists and clinical psychologists.

Psychoanalysts or *psychodynamic therapists* are psychotherapists who use a particular theory of psychotherapy, such as that of Freud or Jung, which places special emphasis on the influence of early experiences, and the impact of these on later relationships. Much emphasis is also put on the client's relationship with the therapist in the room (see also Chapter 3). Treatment can sometimes be open-ended, lasting for many years, although it can be briefer. The focus is on unconscious as well as conscious material, and therapy isn't symptom-focused, being aimed instead at self-development and insight.

Cognitive behaviour therapists use cognitively derived frameworks (often based on experimental research) to understand how a person has developed maladaptive behaviours or thoughts (see Chapter 3). Therapists may follow a manual, which suggests what steps to follow based on research evidence. Therapy involves the client building a collaborative relationship with the therapist to try to test out and establish alternative ways of thinking or behaving, often by completing 'homework'. Focus is normally on the here and now, and on reducing particular symptoms such as low mood or insomnia. Many clinical psychologists integrate some of these techniques into their practice.

Forensic, *educational*, *school*, *occupational*, *sports and exercise*, and *health psychologists* are all qualified psychologists who apply a range of psychological competencies in specific areas of work, or with particular groups of clients: respectively those involved with the criminal justice system, schools and colleges, workplaces, sport, and the wider healthcare system. There are many similarities with clinical psychology, although the focus in each speciality is to work with the particular needs of the different organizations and of their clients. The form and content of training paths also differ to enable practitioners to work effectively in their specific areas of expertise. Often it is the organization that requests the help of the psychologist, not clients themselves.

Social workers, *marriage* and *family therapists* all provide specialist help to clients with a variety of social and interpersonal problems, from housing and welfare to family or marital breakdown and fostering. Some of these therapists make use of psychological models of intervention, for example those working with adoption or mental health services, while others focus on supporting clients through the complexities and practicalities of social security provision.

believe that distress results from a complex set of circumstances, relationships, and patterns of behaviour (which may or may not include individual biological factors), rather than from an organically based mental illness or disease.

When any of us seeks help, we are understood to have reached an impasse of some sort in our lives, and to need some assistance in finding a better way of dealing with or adapting to circumstances. The psychologist's role is to help us to explore what is going on in our lives and to figure out why our previous attempts to solve difficulties may not be working now. Although medication might indeed be helpful for some of us, this is not the psychologist's primary responsibility. Interventions used by clinical psychologists mostly involve observing, talking, and thinking. The psychologist may also ask us to observe things very closely in the here-and-now, inside and outside the therapy session, perhaps trying out new ways of thinking and behaving, in our daily lives or interactions with others. Crucially, all those involved, sometimes including family or carers, will work together to reduce the distress, or to promote wellbeing.

Central to the practice of clinical psychology are individual formulations and treatment plans which are as far as possible based on ideas and methods that have been found to be effective through research, in other words they have a strong evidence base. But psychologists are also acutely aware that problems don't occur in isolation, and that it is very important to understand the context for each individual client.

For example, the behaviour of a child who is labelled as 'difficult' is often best understood by looking at how those around the child are reacting to him, rather than just looking at the child alone. The family may also be under a great deal of strain, maybe because of marital discord or debt. So the training of clinical psychologists also ensures that they are familiar with theories concerning social and family systems as well as those about individual functioning. Put together, this means that psychologists can adapt their interventions to suit a particular person or situation, rather than relying on a manual which specifies what needs to be done, irrespective of the unique person and their particular history.

The different roles of the clinical psychologist

The responsibilities that are carried out by clinical psychologists normally include playing a number of different roles, depending on the needs of the client, and the nature of the organization that the clinical psychologist works for. Typically these roles include that of individual therapist, member of a team of other professionals delivering a service to a specific group of clients, researcher, teacher, supervisor, advisor, and consultant. The underlying *modus operandi* of clinical psychologists when fulfilling these roles is often described as that of the 'scientist-practitioner'. But added to this is the importance of reflecting on how this might work in any individual case, and adapting to or learning from this experience in practice. This is sometimes called being a 'reflective practitioner'. Combining these two ways of working together results in the rather cumbersome but inclusive notion of the clinical psychologist as a 'reflective scientist-practitioner'.

What the term 'reflective scientist-practitioner' means

The following example shows how the clinical psychologist works as a reflective scientist-practitioner: first assessing the difficulty; then developing hypotheses about why it started and why it is still troubling the client; next intervening to change it; then monitoring any changes; and then, if needed, modifying the intervention and repeating the process (see Box 3 showing a clinical psychologist working with a young girl who experiences symptoms of depression).

Box 3 A clinical psychologist helps a young girl who experiences depression

Cassie was a depressed 15-year-old who had harmed herself on several occasions by cutting her arms, and who had been referred for therapy. First, the clinical psychologist carried out an assessment by talking with Cassie and asking her about what has been going on, and also by asking her to complete a variety of psychometric measures (questionnaires) designed to clarify how she thought and felt. These provided an estimate of how severe and wide-ranging the problems were. Next the clinical

(continued)

Box 3 Continued

psychologist developed some hypotheses about what seemed to be causing Cassie to feel depressed and to self-harm. To do this, the clinical psychologist drew upon a number of sources. These included what is known from research about depression and self-harm in young people in general; any recent updates on the topic; the psychologist's own clinical experience of having worked with similar adolescents in the past; and, most importantly, Cassie's unique experience and opinions, as revealed by the assessment. Next, the clinical psychologist discussed these hypotheses with Cassie, and proposed a formulation (see Chapter 3) together with a possible plan for therapy.

With Cassie's agreement, therapy involved encouraging Cassie to express her feelings and exploring her negative beliefs about herself. The final stage, after several months of therapy, involved the clinical psychologist assessing whether the intervention had been effective, by asking Cassie to repeat the psychometric measures to check if things had improved. Cassie was also asked to give feedback on her experience of the intervention, and its effectiveness.

Although clinical psychologists are committed to using approaches that have been supported by evidence (rather than opinion, hearsay, or tradition), being a scientist-practitioner does not mean treating the other person impersonally or unemotionally, like in a classic scientific experiment. In fact, psychological interventions work best when they are based on a warm, trusting, confidential, and mutually respectful personal relationship between the psychologist and client, and where the person seeking help feels secure enough to reveal personal information and to risk making changes. An important role is simply to provide a safe place and opportunity for clients to unburden themselves of distress, so that clients can open up about feelings that are usually avoided.

The term 'simply' used here probably greatly underestimates the importance of this aspect of the clinical psychologist's work.

An essential part of being a reflective scientist-practitioner is a commitment to evaluation. This means assessing as objectively as possible whether the intervention has or has not been successful. If it hasn't, one possibility is that hypotheses about the difficulty were not accurate enough. So the clinical psychologist would then reflect on why—normally by gathering more information, and discussing this with the client. Maybe Cassie's distress (see example in Box 3) was actually being caused by something like a past history of sexual abuse, which she did not initially feel safe enough to reveal. If so, this would result in an alternative hypothesis and probably a revised therapy plan. This process can be repeated until the client's issue is resolved.

The 'reflective' part of being a reflective scientist-practitioner has several implications. As well as carefully matching any particular therapy or theory to the needs of particular clients, the clinical psychologist also needs to be aware of and adapt to the client's cultural background. This doesn't mean the psychologist has to know everything about all cultures. Rather, they need to be prepared to be open-minded and to express respectful curiosity about the client's beliefs. This way the clinical psychologist can avoid acting in ways that might conflict with the client's particular cultural viewpoint. For example, there are differences between different cultural groups about the most appropriate ways of responding to death and bereavement. This needs to be born in mind when working with a bereaved person from another culture, so that the clinical psychologist doesn't make clumsy assumptions about what 'should' happen when someone dies.

A related point is that clinical psychologists shouldn't assume that there is only one side of any story, but should appreciate that there are normally many causes of psychological distress, and many ways of seeing things. For example, it would be unhelpful for a clinical psychologist to 'blame' a parent for a child's behaviour, or 'blame' the child: instead the clinical psychologist would try to understand what is going on to cause the family's unhappiness, including the parent, child, and other contributing factors lying outside the family itself. These could include factors like housing difficulties, poverty, unemployment, or the family's experience of racism—all of which may be part of the problem, even if not strictly 'psychological' or 'mental' in origin. Essentially clinical psychologists are less interested in facts (as seen by, say, a lawyer or detective), than in people's subjective experiences, their 'truth', and what life is like according to them, regardless of other people's perception of it.

A final meaning of being a reflective scientist-practitioner is that clinical psychologists are committed to monitoring the overall effects of their work, exploring in detail what helped and what did not, so that the things they learn from this particular person's therapy or assessment can also be used to benefit others with similar difficulties in future. Sometimes clinical psychologists might participate in large-scale studies, for example by providing data on the outcome of therapy for a national trial on the effectiveness of a new type of treatment. Or sometimes they might systematically collect information about one small aspect of a local service, like investigating how the wording of the appointment letter impacts on the number of people who attend their first appointment. In all cases, clinical psychologists, as reflective scientists, try always to remain open to feedback and the need for continuous professional improvement, gaining more knowledge through further training and study.

Supervision and ethical issues

All clinical psychologists aim to develop professionally respectful and positive attitudes towards those they work with, and therefore take time to reflect on any personal feelings (either negative or excessively positive) that might impede a proper professional relationship. To help them with this, clinical psychologists receive regular supervision, which is not a process of being told what to do by a superior, but rather an opportunity to talk about difficulties and dilemmas with a respected and more experienced colleague. Supervisors aim to offer a safe place where together they and the clinical psychologist can explore any difficulties or dilemmas that emerge in their work (see also Chapter 1).

All professionally registered clinical psychologists are bound by the ethical code of the body that registers them. In the UK this is the Health and Care Professions Council, which also regulates the use of the title 'clinical psychologist', and requires registrants to keep up to date. In the USA, this is the American Psychological Association; with a Board of Psychology in every state, who issues registrants with licenses to practice; and requirements for continuing education to keep informed about developments in the field. Such codes, together with professional organizations like the British Psychological Society (BPS), are designed to promote high standards amongst their membership and to protect clients.

For instance, according to the BPS Code of Conduct and Ethics, clinical psychologists must treat everybody equally, regardless of age, gender, occupation, sexual orientation, skin colour, etc. The clinical psychologist's underlying professional responsibility is (wherever possible) to promote people's autonomy, according to the client's own unique set of values and priorities. In other words, the client's needs, choices, and values should determine what happens, not the clinical psychologist's.

Psychologists must not exploit the close trusting relationship that often develops between themselves and their clients for their own personal gratification or financial gain beyond any agreed professional fee. It is also important that clinical psychologists do not impose their own views, however subtly, onto the person they are working with. For example, although a clinical psychologist might not hold any religious belief themselves, or be a committed

Box 4 A clinical psychologist facing a moral dilemma

Mike, a colleague of ours, was once asked to provide psychological therapy for Bill, a man who reported acute anxiety about doing certain tasks in his workplace. Bill described regularly having incapacitating palpitations and panic attacks at home prior to setting out for assignments, and wanted psychological help to control his anxiety. This seemed a reasonable request, exactly the kind of thing a clinical psychologist can help with. Mike was just starting to develop a treatment plan for Bill, when he asked Bill for more details of the work involved. It emerged that Bill was part of a gang of criminal house burglars, and that he felt anxious before breaking and entering into other people's homes! Mike told us he felt it was ethically appropriate to decline to provide Bill with psychological treatment for his pre-burgling anxieties.

member of a different church, they should be respectful of the other person's religious beliefs. Having said that, psychologists don't have to act contrary to their own consciences or morals (see Box 4).

Working with colleagues and systems

Although some clinical psychologists work completely independently (e.g. those engaged in private practice), and manage their own lists of clients, the majority of clinical psychologists work in healthcare organizations in close association with other professionals, such as psychiatrists, neurologists, occupational therapists, rehabilitation therapists, social workers, psychotherapists, and psychiatric nurses. This implies three things.

First, the clinical psychologist needs to be able to collaborate closely with colleagues who have been trained in different ways, using very different views and assumptions about the best way to work with clients. This requires flexibility, good interpersonal skills, an appreciation of the importance of teamwork, and recognition that multiple perspectives often co-exist.

Second, the comparatively small size of the clinical psychology profession means that we often have to work through other staff, helping others to deliver psychological interventions rather than doing so ourselves. This is sometimes known as 'working indirectly'. For example, a clinical psychologist working within a psychiatric inpatient ward might develop a programme to help staff encourage a very distressed patient to take her medication more regularly (as part of a plan to enable her eventual discharge from hospital). It would, however, be the doctors and nurses who would actually implement the plan. Or a clinical psychologist (who is part of a team specializing in work with families who offer foster care), might most usefully help a particularly challenging family indirectly by helping the team to think more clearly about what is happening within the family. The psychologist might also offer support to staff members who are themselves finding it hard to work with the family or the child. Or a clinical psychologist (working in an older people's care home where residents appear depressed and withdrawn) might encourage the nurses to move chairs in the lounge area from rows (where no-one can easily chat) into small groups, hence encouraging conversation between residents. Thus the clinical psychologist may be more effective in promoting the older people's wellbeing by changing the staff's behaviour and ideas, than by working directly themselves with the individual clients.

Third, working for any organization (large or small) means taking some interest in how organizations work. This inevitably involves the need to attend meetings, read official paperwork, etc., and deal with some degree of bureaucracy. But it also offers opportunities to shape those organizations and bring about productive change. For example, many clinical psychologists develop management and leadership skills that enable them to promote psychological care within their organizations. Some have also taken up senior leadership roles, and have had a major impact on how the whole organization runs, for example by encouraging a hospital to take much closer account of the views of clients in how services should be organized.

Where clinical psychologists work

Very simply, clinical psychologists work wherever best suits their clients. This could mean perching on the edge of a bed within a busy in-patient hospital ward or hospice, if, for example, someone needs psychological care following an emergency admission. Or it could mean finding space within a care home or residential facility, possibly seeing a client together with other members of the staff team. Although some clinical psychologists visit clients in their homes, most clients attend day or outpatient services, and will see the clinical psychologist in the psychologist's own office where confidential discussions are most possible. Clinical psychologists working with children or young people often use comfortable rooms or play areas, stocked with toys and pictures, while families may be seen in specially constructed suites, sometimes with two-way mirrors allowing a number of clinical psychologists to work together.

Group sessions can be held within hospital settings, schools, community offices, or church buildings. Or a clinical psychologist may be part of an out-reach service where they will work wherever the client is most comfortable: for example, a café or park bench, where the psychologist might meet with an adolescent who is too apprehensive to come into any closer contact with health professionals. Clinical psychologists who work in private practice normally use their own office space located in either a private clinic or suite of rooms, possibly shared with other private practitioners. Recently it has also become more common practice to conduct sessions by telephone or Skype when a client is unable to visit the clinical psychologist in person (see Chapter 7).

Getting to see a clinical psychologist

There are a number of ways people can get in touch with a clinical psychologist if they want psychological help. If the clinical psychologist works in private practice, and offers their services directly to the public, people can simply call and request an appointment for an assessment. The psychologist will probably advertise, listing contact details in a professional directory, indicating their qualifications, fees, approach to work, theories used, and area of special expertise. Quite often however their contact details will be handed on by word of mouth by others who have previously found them helpful.

When the clinical psychologist works for a community clinic or in a managed healthcare setting, clients would normally be referred by another professional such as a doctor, nurse, care home worker, teacher, or social worker (although some services also accept self-referral). The person making the referral will have already met the client and might suggest to the clinical psychologist what kind of help they think is needed, or will request help for a particular problem. When the psychologist is part of a multi-disciplinary team—for example, an eating disorder team, assessment unit for pre-school children, or rehabilitation unit—the clinical psychologist may simply work as part of a standard comprehensive service.

The rest of this VSI will outline the key elements of how clinical psychologists work in practice in their roles as therapists, researchers, teachers, supervisors, or service leaders. First, however, we will have a look at the kinds of people who may seek and gain from the help provided by clinical psychology.

Chapter 2
From the cradle to the grave

Clinical psychologists work with an enormous variety of people and this chapter will provide some examples. Clients come from across the entire lifespan, from birth to death, and from all walks and stages of life. This includes children and families, adults with mental health difficulties, older people, people with intellectual disabilities, people with physical health challenges (like disability or chronic illness), and groups with particular needs, such as prisoners, members of the armed forces, and refugees. There is no such person as a typical client, although those who benefit most from psychological interventions are probably those who attend by choice and are prepared to think psychologically about themselves. That is, they are willing to spend time examining themselves, their behaviour, emotions, and personal beliefs, and don't simply want a straightforward medical solution, or quick fix for their problems or questions.

From infancy onwards, people learn and develop as they navigate their way through life, changing psychologically as they age physically. Clinical psychologists make sense of their clients' experiences by using a whole lifespan approach. This means that what is happening now is understood to be at least partly a consequence of what happened before, and that normal age-related transitions (such as the birth of siblings, moving schools, leaving home, gaining (or losing) employment, becoming a parent, retirement, or bereavement) are likely to be highly significant for people's ongoing development, health, and satisfaction.

Clinical psychologists always work through discussion or collaboration, and gain active agreement from their clients, although consent for some people (e.g. young children, or those with restricted ability to consent such as people with advanced dementia or severe intellectual disabilities) may be obtained from others (i.e. families and carers). Most work is done directly with the client, although as noted in Chapter 1, sometimes interventions are carried out indirectly, by providing guidance, teaching, or supervision to staff members or other helpers. Many therapies for children or older people are conducted collaboratively with parents, families, or carers, who are usually in a better position to bring about sustainable changes than a clinical psychologist working alone with the client would be.

Children, young people, and families

Childhood is the time of maximum psychological change, and the learning, attachment patterns, and coping mechanisms acquired here will all have ramifications throughout life, for good or ill. All children will inevitably experience some distress at some stage, as they learn to separate from parents and deal with the unavoidable knocks of life. But most children are adaptable, and only a minority will experience major problems. These usually (but not always) result from disruptions in or inconsistent parenting, or adverse circumstances. No upbringing is perfect, but some children have very negative experiences like neglect, emotional or physical abuse, or trauma. The teenage years are a time of transition, and although most young people cope well and maintain good relationships during this time with their parents, peers, and teachers, some will struggle. A combination of social, developmental, economic, physical, and hormonal changes sometimes combine to result in psychological distress or instability.

There are five major types of difficulty for which children and young people are typically referred or seek help from clinical psychology: behavioural; emotional; problems with eating; psychosis; and physical/developmental disorders.

Behavioural problems include sleeping difficulties, being excessively defiant, or being very hard to control. The latter two problems have been reported in between 10 and 20 per cent of young people at any one time. These are best addressed jointly with parents, for example through parent training. If left untreated, there is a risk of later substance misuse or involvement in illegal activities.

Emotional problems, including anxiety, obsessional or compulsive behaviours, low mood and depression, may affect up to one in three young people at some stage, most of whom don't have access to effective professional help. Cognitive behaviour therapy (CBT) (see Chapter 4) can be helpful, although both family therapy and interpersonal psychotherapy can help too.

Eating disorders (including anorexia nervosa, bulimia nervosa, and binge eating disorder) occur in around 1–2 per cent of young people, often first showing up in the teenage years. Anorexia in particular can be extremely serious, even life-threatening. Treatment generally involves some variant of CBT or family therapy (see Box 5).

Psychosis (thinking, behaving, and feeling in ways which are maladaptive and differ very significantly from what most of us understand to be reality) is rare in children, but early warning signs can emerge in the mid-teens. Treatment is often medication-based, but increasingly, early intervention teams are being established, which work by using psychological therapies and providing support for families.

Box 5 A clinical psychologist works with a girl with eating problems

Thirteen-year-old Polly was a friendly but quiet girl who had previously enjoyed school and a range of after-school activities. She was taken to the doctor by her mother who said that, apparently out of the blue, Polly had started worrying excessively about her appearance. She told her parents that she had been teased at school about being 'fat', and had started restricting her food intake and exercising regularly. She said she felt stupid, useless, and unattractive. Over time she lost a significant amount of weight and was referred to the local eating disorder service, which she initially refused to attend. The service then arranged a short series of sessions with a clinical psychologist to try to build her self-esteem, and to encourage her to see a dietician in order to develop healthier eating patterns. During these sessions the psychologist helped Polly to think about the function of food in her life, and what eating or not eating might communicate about being loved, being seen, and growing up.

Finally, psychological difficulties can arise when young people need to learn to adapt to physical disabilities or chronic physical health problems (see Box 6 for an example of an adolescent with diabetes). Developmental problems such as learning difficulties and autism (or autistic spectrum disorder) tend to emerge in childhood (affecting between 4 and 1 per cent, respectively, of school-age children). Developmental problems need careful psychological assessment using a variety of cognitive, behavioural, physical, and neurological measures, and are often addressed by multi-disciplinary teams including doctors, nurses, clinical psychologists, teachers, social workers, occupational therapists, physiotherapists, and families themselves.

Although the child or young person's behaviour is usually the reason for the referral to services, therapy often includes parents,

Box 6 A clinical psychologist working with a young person with diabetes

Bobby, now aged 15, first received help from clinical psychology when, aged 6, he was diagnosed with Type-1 diabetes. Bobby had become very fearful of medical procedures involved with managing his diabetes, so the clinical psychologist was asked to assist him in talking about his fears, and to reduce his anxiety about needles and blood tests. This was helpful, but to respond fully to Bobby's needs it was also crucial to work with Elaine, Bobby's mother, who was herself very distressed and unable to reassure Bobby effectively. It emerged that although Elaine had looked forward to Bobby's birth, the delivery had been difficult, with many medical complications, resulting in Elaine having recurrent traumatic memories. These memories resurfaced after Bobby's diabetes diagnosis and Elaine said she felt that somehow she has been responsible for Bobby's health problems. The hospital arranged for another clinical psychologist to provide extra support for Elaine, helping her to manage the traumatic memories, and to support the wider family as they learned how to respond effectively to Bobby's ongoing health needs.

Over subsequent years, like many young people with physical health conditions, Bobby struggled with having to manage his diet carefully, especially when, as a teenager, he didn't want to appear different from friends, or to have to avoid foods or alcohol which might upset his glucose levels. This led to frequent arguments with his mother Elaine. Again a clinical psychologist was asked to help Bobby as he struggled with the contrasting needs of managing his health, his wish to become more independent while maintaining his relationship with his mother, and his desire to fit in with his peers.

teachers, or carers, rather than focusing just on the young person. Early intervention is important since, if left untreated, these problems can persist and may have longer term implications for the young person's life trajectory and health.

People of working age

People of working age (18–65 years old) probably constitute the majority of those who consult clinical psychologists. The reasons vary hugely. First are those who want to improve their relationships with others both socially and professionally, or those who want to gain self-understanding, perhaps because they are themselves undertaking training as a psychological practitioner.

Second are people who, sometimes triggered by life changes like having a child, not being able to have a child, starting or ending employment, starting or ending relationships, moving house, and so on, experience overwhelming feelings of depression, anxiety, confusion, or anger. Or sometimes such feelings occur 'out of the blue'. They can significantly impair the person's enjoyment of life and relationships (even though in many cases people still manage to cope reasonably well at home and work).

A third group are those who have experienced a devastating major mental health problem, such as psychosis or complex trauma, affecting all aspects of their lives. Finally some groups of people may have specific needs for psychological help which are connected with their particular (but very different) life circumstances, such as involvement with the criminal justice system, being in the armed forces, or being a refugee or asylum seeker. Clinical psychologists working with these groups often seek further training to ensure that they have a thorough understanding of people's specific needs in such environments.

These sub-divisions are rather arbitrary, and the numbers seeking help in each grouping will vary across cultures. For example, in some developing countries, where there aren't many clinical psychologists in state-funded employment and costs are high, the majority of clinical psychologist work with clients who present with serious and enduring mental health difficulties, rather than with the more common mental health difficulties. The reverse is probably the case in some wealthier countries where most clients are seen privately.

Being curious: wanting to understand and develop yourself further

First, for some people, seeing a clinical psychologist offers the possibility of gaining enhanced self-understanding. This is important for all mental health professionals as part of their own professional development. Others may consult a clinical psychologist in order to explore and find a way to resolve personal uncertainties or dilemmas. The client is not 'ill' in the medical sense of the word, but they sense things could be better at work, home, or in relationships (see the example in Box 7). For instance, the client might be intrigued by how their upbringing has impacted upon them, and want a confidential place to examine past experiences, so they can try to understand why (for example) they seem stuck in certain patterns of behaviour, and maybe improve their self-confidence.

Seeing a clinical psychologist when you have no major emotional problems is more common in some countries than in others. Clinical psychologists in some parts of South America, for example, have a longstanding tradition of providing psychological therapy for clients who wish to understand themselves better, find purpose in life, and/or improve their quality of life—looking for positive changes that will promote a sense of personal growth and accomplishment. Therapy is seen as self-care, similar to having a personal trainer who works with you on your physical health.

Box 7 Nicky seeks help for her relationship difficulties

Nicky, a single parent in her late 30s, approached a clinical psychologist for help because she felt trapped and stuck in her personal relationships. Nicky had become pregnant in her early 20s and had lived temporarily with the child's father, but the relationship had not worked out, ending when he became physically violent. Nicky had a reasonably good job in local government and was able to move out with her daughter into a small flat of their own, where she managed well and built up a circle of women friends. However, her relationships with men troubled her: each man she dated seemed to be perfect initially but would then let her down, or take advantage, for example borrowing large sums of money that were never repaid. Nicky felt sure she was always choosing the wrong sort of partner or doing something wrong, and wanted to understand this: was she fated always to have failed relationships? Although she did not currently feel particularly distressed, she decided to consult a clinical psychologist privately to try to understand what was happening, why she felt trapped in a repeated cycle, and how she might alter this in the future.

When life suddenly throws you off balance

The second (probably largest) group of people of working age who consult clinical psychologists are those with relatively common, but nonetheless very distressing, mental health difficulties. These include emotionally upsetting feelings, behaviours, or thoughts that significantly impair people's enjoyment of life, turning some aspects of their existence into a daily grind, a private misery, or a seemingly endless roller coaster of fear. We now know that there are huge numbers of people who, despite living ordinary lives, making relationships, and managing the demands of work or bringing up a family, also experience high levels of personal distress. Some may make use of substances such as drugs and alcohol to deal with or avoid such feelings. Clinical psychologists aim to help those who feel like this to explore alternative, less harmful, coping skills, and to develop better strategies to deal with overwhelming feelings.

Generally speaking, this type of distress gets labelled as one of the following: panic, generalized anxiety, phobias, post-traumatic stress, obsessive compulsive behaviours or thoughts, depression, eating disorders, substance mis-use, family and social relationship difficulties, or sexual difficulties. And of course several problems may well co-exist. There are various examples of common mental

Box 8 Stuart seeks help for his anxiety-related symptoms

Stuart loved his two daughters, calling them the shining jewels in his perfect life. However, his inner life was a nightmare: he was plagued by the idea that he might one day accidentally or purposefully harm his children by running them over. To prevent this, he developed a complex set of rituals, like saying a series of mantras out loud while driving his car, checking local traffic reports, and returning to where he had driven that day to make sure no accidents to children had taken place. These rituals and actions, which he felt had to be performed regularly to neutralize his thoughts and prevent the awful events taking place, gradually took over his life. In desperation Stuart consulted a clinical psychologist who, having assessed the actual risk of harm to the children as minimal, eventually helped Stuart to understand the difference between thoughts and actions: having a thought does not actually cause it to happen.

health disorders in this VSI, such as Barbara's phobia of dogs and Abdul's fear of noise (probably linked to trauma) described in Chapter 3, and Stuart's anxieties, described in Box 8 in this chapter.

When problems seem to take over everything

The third group comprises those with enduring mental health problems, traditionally labelled as 'mentally ill'. For many years clinical psychologists did not play a major role in the treatment of people diagnosed by psychiatrists as suffering from serious mental illness, that is from conditions such as schizophrenia, bi-polar disorder, personality disorder, and psychosis (although psychologists did play a significant role in their assessment). These mental illnesses were thought to be caused by faults in the brain, and were either seen as completely untreatable or only treatable by medication within mental hospitals.

More recently however clinical psychologists have become involved in managing common symptoms and difficulties that occur as a consequence of the mental health problem (such as irritability with partner/family/boss; isolation, lack of self-care/risky behaviour). They have also started to listen carefully to the accounts given by patients of their thoughts and experience, discovering that some apparently meaningless symptoms, such as paranoia (feeling you are special or singled out in some way) may actually make some sense given the person's circumstances. In addition, clinical psychology researchers have shown that many so-called 'normal' people also experience unusual things (such as hearing voices), not just those who have been labelled 'mentally ill'. Clinical psychologists have thereby re-drawn the treatment map: early intervention, talking treatments (see Box 9 for a clinical example), and teaching families how to reduce stress have made a huge difference for many of those with major mental health problems. This has helped many people towards stabilization, maintenance, and sometimes recovery.

Box 9 Steve hears voices and gets support from a clinical psychologist

Steve had been diagnosed some years earlier by psychiatric services as suffering from severe mental health problems, possibly schizophrenia. Steve, who was unemployed, lived at home with his parents, and they gradually noticed he had stopped seeing friends or going out. He also stopped washing, didn't sleep much, and was spending more and more time awake at night on his computer. He explained to his parents that he had to work on complex philosophical questions, the solution to which he was sure would prove to be a major theological breakthrough, of great significance to the world. His re-admission to psychiatric hospital followed a couple of episodes where he had behaved very oddly, culminating in him attempting to climb onto the roof of the house apparently on the instruction of devils.

After a few weeks in hospital and a change in medication, Steve agreed to meet the ward clinical psychologist and told her that he was forced to obey the voices' commands, but also that he was terrified of them, convinced they proved he was irrecoverably mad. The clinical psychologist established a collaborative relationship with Steve, and encouraged him to think about his voices in less threatening ways, aiming to reduce the distress associated with them. Working with the ward team, the clinical psychologist also helped Steve to make progress towards his personal goals, including re-gaining employment and re-contacting his friends, thus enabling his eventual discharge from hospital.

Surviving trauma and challenging circumstances

The final grouping comprises a minority of people whose difficulties are inextricably linked to the state or legal system, or to wider social problems. This includes people in prison, in institutional care, in the armed forces, or those who are refugees or asylum seekers, all of whom may face particular emotional challenges. Involvement in the criminal justice system, or being subject to restrictions and/or persecution, unfortunately often contributes significantly to people's emotional problems.

First, we know that people in forensic settings such as prison or special high security hospitals may themselves have been traumatized, abused, neglected, or victims of crime, and will probably have engaged in (or been subject to) risky, anti-social, and violent behaviour or situations in the past. The prison or secure hospital can itself be a traumatic and dangerous place where inmates are surrounded by other troubled people and stressed staff, and are without regular contact with family or friends. Inevitably this population has high levels of emotional distress. UK statistics, for example, show that more than 70 per cent of the prison population has two or more diagnosable mental health disorders.

Common problems include poor anger management, substance misuse, and difficulties with interpersonal relationships. Some require detention in secure hospitals because of the danger they pose to themselves and others, and this group has many additional needs. Enduring mental health difficulties such as psychosis or complex trauma are relatively common amongst people in the criminal justice system; half of all prisoners have a serious mental illness (according to US statistics). Psychological work to resolve any associated mental health problems in forensic settings is normally complex and lengthy, and is aimed at protecting society by reducing the chances of the person repeating their offending behaviour while also supporting re-integration of the person back into society.

Second, clinical psychology services are increasingly being provided within the military: for example, the Department of Veterans' Affairs is now the largest employer of clinical psychologists in the USA. During the course of deployment, military personnel are often exposed to intense trauma and stress. This can lead to symptoms of post-traumatic stress disorder (PTSD) such as irritability, anger, and violence. People who suffer from PTSD sometimes try to numb their feelings by using drugs and alcohol, or by being excessively involved in work or video games. Here psychologists can provide marital or family therapy with the aim of reducing interpersonal conflict, and promoting understanding or social support. Other clinical psychologists also work on other aspects of military life, such as selection and training.

Third, we are becoming increasingly aware that clinical psychological work is needed with refugees and asylum seekers, many of whom may have survived great physical and mental challenges including war-related trauma, violence, re-location, and multiple losses. This is often complicated by the challenges of integration into a new culture and society. Refugees must contend with new language, social norms, and expectations while being isolated and without the support of families and friends. Common forms of distress in this group include substance misuse, relationship breakdown, and depression, plus symptoms of PTSD (particularly re-experiencing past traumatic events in the present, emotional numbing, nightmares, and avoidance of anything that is a reminder of the migration or other trauma). Therapies that can be helpful are similar to those used with other psychologically distressed people, with special emphasis on social integration and re-building of lives.

Older people

Most of us know that, compared with previous centuries, we are all now living much longer, and the proportion of older people in the population has increased significantly. This should be a cause for celebration. However, particularly in Western societies, older people are often not valued as highly as younger people; services may be patchier, and attitudes less optimistic. Sadly this time of life also tends to bring a number of losses such as loss of occupation and perceived status, separation from children or moving from the family home, and bereavement following the deaths of spouse, friends, and family (see Box 10 for a clinical

Box 10 A clinical psychologist helps an older person to become less isolated

Mary, a retired teacher in her late 60s, was widowed and had two grown up children: Peter, who was in the middle of a messy divorce, and Helen, who lived abroad. The clinical psychologist was asked to meet Mary because her doctor felt Mary wasn't coping well with feelings of anxiety and depression. Some months previously, Mary had been driving home after visiting Peter, and was so pre-occupied by thoughts about him that she had a minor car accident (although no-one was injured). Subsequently she had avoided going back to the town where Peter lived, feeling both upset for herself and guilty about not helping Peter more. She told the clinical psychologist that she had almost completely abandoned driving or going out, and was spending most of her time sitting worrying at home.

The clinical psychologist asked Mary to describe her experiences and feelings, and outline what she wanted from therapy. Mary said this was, first, to start driving again so she could help Peter; and, second, to feel less depressed and worried. Together Mary and the clinical psychologist developed a plan to reduce Mary's distress. The clinical psychologist was aware that a very human tendency after an unpleasant experience (like having an accident) is to try to avoid the possibility of such a thing happening again, for example by avoiding going to places similar to where the accident happened. Clinical psychological research has shown, however, that avoiding similar places or activities paradoxically further adds to the difficulty. This is because although avoidance temporarily makes you feel better, you never learn that the place or activity is probably not as dangerous as you fear.

So therapy with Mary started with helping her to describe the accident in detail, and then in very small stages, to start driving again: small distances at first but gradually building her

(continued)

Box 10 Continued

confidence to tackle longer journeys. As she gained trust in the
psychologist, Mary also talked about her loneliness and irrational
sense of guilt about Peter's family problems. The clinical
psychologist then worked with Mary to take steps to reduce her
isolation, for example encouraging her to join a class to learn IT
skills so that she could communicate online with Helen (the
daughter living abroad); and to make contact with some of her
ex-colleagues from her teaching days. Gradually Mary became
more confident and started going out again, both seeing Peter
and volunteering at a local school.

example). Chronic and acute physical health challenges increase,
for example arthritis, diabetes, stroke, cancer, or heart disease,
all of which might lead to dependency on others. Many older
people are involved in caring for others, particularly spouses,
who are unwell. We might expect these life stresses to warrant
psychological input, but in our clinical work we have noticed that
many older people are unused to asking for help or addressing
their emotional experience, seeing their problems as expected
consequences of ageing. They may believe in self-reliance, hard
work, and the need to keep a 'stiff upper lip'.

Traditionally there are two main types of mental health problems
common in older age: 'organic' and 'functional'. Organic problems
include a variety of progressive cognitive (brain) changes, ranging
from minor cognitive impairment to dementia (see Box 11 for a
clinical example), while functional problems include anxiety,
depression, post-traumatic stress, psychosis, and eating disorders,
all of which can be triggered by life changes. Clinical psychology
services for 'organic' problems include careful neuro-psychological
assessment, followed by direct or indirect interventions with the
older person and their family. Clinical psychologists might also

Box 11 An elderly couple struggling with confusion and memory problems

Mr and Mrs Spencer lived in a small village some way from their grown-up children, and had enjoyed reasonably good health until their late 70s. However Mrs Spencer had started to notice her husband was getting forgetful and was losing interest in activities that he had previously been passionate about, such as his garden and local football club. Following the sudden death of his oldest friend, Mr Spencer had become more withdrawn and sometimes seemed confused.

At the request of the local older people's community health service, a clinical psychologist carried out psychometric testing to assess whether Mr Spencer was suffering from depression or the onset of a dementing process. It was clear that he was depressed, so the team set up a programme of activities with him so that he could re-connect with things that he used to enjoy. Nevertheless, his abilities continued to decline, so the team eventually concluded he was indeed suffering from dementia as well. His wife was determined to care for him at home, which she did for a few months, but became exhausted and distressed, refusing all offers of respite care.

Another member of the clinical psychology team then offered her a number of sessions to help her talk through her distress about the changes in her husband, and to encourage her to accept some help for herself from local services. The psychologist also met with the couple's children, who had not realized the extent of Mr Spencer's difficulties, but who then started to visit more regularly. Eventually Mrs Spencer and the family were able to reach the decision that Mr Spencer would move into a local care home for specialist care.

establish specific treatment programmes such as memory clinics for mild memory loss, or may facilitate support groups for carers of people with dementia.

Psychological services for 'functional' problems are similar to those for younger adults but need to take into account the increased chances of physical ill health or frailty, together with the increased number of life events likely to be impacting on older people. In addition, the organizations or systems around the person, such as care home staff, neighbours, partner or family members, probably also need to be involved in any intervention.

People with intellectual disabilities

Some people struggle with daily tasks from very early on in their lives. About 1 to 2 per cent of the population worldwide have intellectual disabilities that originate before the age of 18. This means that they experience significant limitations in both intellectual functioning (IQ) and in adaptive behaviour (everyday social and practical skills needed to function in society). Research also shows that they are more likely than the rest of us to be bullied and abused, and to have poor physical health or disabilities. While clinical psychologists in some parts of the world provide dedicated services to people with intellectual disability (sometimes known as 'mental retardation' or 'learning disability'), not all clinical psychologists do so. In the UK, for example, this is a standard part of training and service provision, but this is not the case in the USA.

In our society, people with intellectual disabilities are often devalued and not given enough opportunities for developing their skills. However, many psychologists are committed to their value as human beings and their rights to have choices about their lives. Many people with mild intellectual disabilities in fact live successfully in the community, and manage very well with the routine challenges of life, although they may struggle with complex or unexpected demands, and need support from time to time. Others with more severe disabilities find it hard to communicate or to care for themselves at all; this group often needs support from others for most of their lives.

In many instances, the role of clinical psychologists is to work with those who care for intellectually disabled people, whether in families, care homes, or institutions (see Box 12 for a clinical example). The psychologist may, for example, help staff to use behavioural management techniques in response to challenging behaviour, such as someone making inappropriate approaches to staff, or disrupting others' social activities. An often-used approach is functional analysis, a procedure which attempts to uncover what a person is getting out of a behaviour within a particular social context, and why it continues.

Box 12 A clinical psychologist supports staff working with a young man with intellectual disabilities

Ramon was a young man with severe intellectual disabilities who suddenly started causing a great deal of noisy disturbance in his residence. Staff were increasingly annoyed by this and 'blamed' Ramon for being a nuisance, requesting the clinical psychologist to come and help them control Ramon's behaviour. But after spending some time in the residence, the clinical psychologist observed variations in when the disturbances happened. When another, more needy, resident (who had just moved in) was receiving attention, the previously attentive staff team would pay less attention to Ramon. It appeared that shouting was Ramon's only way of regaining staff attention.

The clinical psychologist alerted the staff team to this pattern, and together they worked out alternative ways of reacting to Ramon that did not undermine their confidence as staff, but which also allowed them to pay attention to both residents as

(continued)

Box 12 Continued

needed. This included working with the other resident outside Ramon's line of sight, and giving Ramon a picture schedule and simplified clock that both explained when his turn would come, and reassured him that he wouldn't be forgotten. The clinical psychologist also delivered a staff training programme on 'behaviour as communication', showing how to interpret challenging behaviour in this client group. Following this, the staff team said they could appreciate that Ramon was not doing things 'just to annoy us', and became more curious about what residents were trying to say through their behaviour.

A variety of forms of psychological therapy may also be offered, although probably with modifications, given that intellectually disabled people may have difficulty understanding some abstract ideas. There may also be memory limitations, and a possible confusion about interpersonal boundaries (who is a friend? who is a staff member? what do I talk about with whom? and who can I touch or play with?) that need careful management. Family therapy can be used, for example, to help shift a family who are feeling stuck; to alter some unhelpful ways of thinking about their disabled family member; or to help the family appreciate the person's potential for developing further skills.

People with physical health or neurological problems

A rapidly growing group of people who receive help from clinical psychology are those whose primary difficulties arise from a physical health or neurological condition, and who require extensive or prolonged medical treatment. These include people who experience chronic pain, have a life-threatening illness such as cancer or heart disease, those who have had strokes or neuro-degenerative disorders, and those who have had an accident resulting in spinal injury or other major disability. As medical treatments improve, and more people survive conditions that were previously fatal, new challenges arise for patients and their families. The focus shifts from recovery to rehabilitation: adjusting to the new reality of living with major disabilities, chronic pain, or loss of physical or mental functioning.

The approach most commonly used with these patients is the 'biopsychosocial'. This means paying attention to people's physical health (including their hormonal, physiological, and brain functions) *and* their social context (their family, work, leisure, community), *and* any psychological issues. This awareness is important for all clinical psychologists, but is particularly relevant for those working with neurological symptoms or health problems, where much of the focus is understandably on the medical diagnosis, and where people may be very unwell or seriously disabled.

Research from a biopsychosocial perspective has shown that patients' subjective experience of their health condition, and even their rate of recovery, can be significantly influenced by their emotional state and beliefs. When someone is diagnosed with a physical health condition, such as cancer or heart disease, this obviously has a psychological impact while the person adapts to this new information.

Sometimes this can result in high levels of anxiety and depression, often in anticipation of future distress. Besides causing suffering, this can reduce the person's motivation to adhere to treatment regimes. Clinical psychologists can, however, work with such patients, helping them to discover that their initial appraisal of the situation (that the future is hopelessly gloomy) may be one-sided, and that there are in fact many resources available to help manage both this distress and the illness. These resources might include the person's existing relationships and skills, as well as support available from the hospital and the person's family or community.

An example is a young woman who is newly diagnosed with cancer, and who may feel so despairing and hopeless that she withdraws from family and friends into inactivity and depression. By helping her to focus on adaptive ways of coping, and to use problem solving techniques, the clinical psychologist can help the young woman and her family to find a new way of coping and thriving psychologically, alongside her medical treatment. Such psychological therapies can literally be lifesavers, as people are helped to move from a state of hopelessness and despair to living their lives as fully as possible.

People may also need help with the management of side effects of medication or chemotherapy, for instance fatigue and sleep difficulties. This can improve the person's wellbeing, fitness, and resilience, and ultimately enhance the potential effectiveness of the treatment. Some clinical psychologists work with patients at the end of their lives who are receiving palliative care. Here the aim is to enhance the person's remaining quality of life, manage pain, and maximize the chances of a well-managed death from the point of view of both the patient and their family.

Aside from working with chronic life-threatening illnesses such as cancer, some clinical psychologists choose to work in neuropsychology with people who have had an acquired brain injury, such as that resulting from an accident, from an illness such as meningitis, or from developmental pathology such as a stroke or brain tumour. Such damage can cause major disruption to people's lives and is often accompanied by distressing physical disabilities or neurological effects, for example loss of coordination, seizures, or fatigue. The cognitive disabilities experienced include lack of attention and concentration, memory losses, and difficulties in planning or problem solving. There can also be mood disturbances including depression, anger, frustration, and loss of confidence. In addition, the person may have lost employment and experienced marital/family breakdown as a consequence of the injury.

The role of clinical psychology in neuropsychology varies according to the needs of the individual. Broadly speaking, psychologists tend to work in either acute settings, where their role is mostly to contribute to the assessment and the consequences of a brain injury, or in rehabilitation settings where their role is mostly to promote recovery and help patients and their families to manage the effects of cognitive and behavioural problem. Some conditions happen suddenly (e.g. head injury following a car accident) and may be followed by a period of rehabilitation and recovery, while others are progressive (such as multiple sclerosis) and require increasing levels of support. Patients in acute settings are often physically very unwell, and will be undergoing numerous other medical procedures simultaneously with the psychological assessment.

Psychological assessment (which may be lengthy) should give more information on the extent of the brain damage, how generalized the damage is, what the person's strengths and weaknesses are, and what other pre-existing factors (such as depression) may also play a role. The purpose of the assessment is to identify the extent of the brain injury, which often can't be gauged by a brain scan. Therapy may be provided in some instances, for example helping someone to manage to cope with acute anxiety while undergoing complex medical procedures and brain scans such as CT (computerized tomography) or MRI (magnetic resonance imaging).

In rehabilitation settings, the clinical psychologist's primary aim is to maximize the person's chances of maintaining independence, and to support their ability to continue to play a full part in their family, employment, or community. Work focuses on clarifying the extent of the disability, identifying potential strengths, and finding potential ways of working constructively towards managing long-term changes in functioning. For example, the clinical psychologist may help the patient to use electronic aids to manage severe memory impairment (see Box 13 for a clinical example).

Box 13 A clinical psychologist helps a couple manage after the husband's stroke

Roger was a 63-year-old retired head teacher, who had been very active professionally and socially post-retirement, having been treasurer of a local bowling club. One night, when having a drink at the club, he suffered a stroke. The staff called for an ambulance and following a brief hospital stay, Roger was sent home. As part of routine follow-up, medical doctors referred him for a neuro-psychological assessment to help determine the stroke's impact on his ability to function cognitively. Roger and his wife attended three meetings, detailing his current difficulties. It became clear that they both struggled with Roger's sudden deterioration. He had become highly irritable, having even pushed his wife away roughly on several occasions.

Comprehensive tests of his memory and cognitive and emotional functioning revealed his poor memory for new verbal information, and slowed speed of information processing. He also suffered from word-finding problems. Measures of depression and anxiety indicated he had low mood and was highly anxious in social situations. The clinical psychologist hypothesized that Roger's anxiety was linked to fear of another stroke, and his belief that others would think him stupid because of his poor memory and problems findings words. His poor memory for conversation also contributed to his anxiety in social situations. Roger's high level of irritability was directed at his wife because she tended to speak quickly, interrupt him, and speak for him. His low mood was associated with poor memory, loss of status at his school, loss of his role as breadwinner, and loss of his hobbies.

Together with the clinical psychologist, Roger chose the following goals: 1. To feel less anxious by gradually increasing the amount of time spent away from home, in supermarkets or shops; 2. To manage poor memory by asking people to slow down when talking, noting important points in his electronic diary, and looking at his diary over breakfast every day; 3. To feel less irritated by his wife by 'reminding' her not to interrupt or speak for him, and telling his wife about his feelings; 4. To feel less depressed by going to the Stroke Group at their local health centre twice weekly, and returning to the bowling club committee as an ordinary member; 5. To improve his arm and leg strength by practising his exercises twice daily.

A few months later Roger was able to visit the local supermarket with his wife without anxiety, and reported that he was forgetting fewer important tasks—using his electronic diary to good effect. Also Roger's wife reported that she had become more aware of jumping in, and that there had been fewer arguments over the last month. Roger had also been regularly practising his physical exercises and appeared pleased at his improved strength in his arm and leg.

The injured person's family will probably also be distressed and in need of help, as they learn to live with a relative who may show significant changes in personality and ability, resulting from their injury.

These are just some of the many scenarios in which people at different stages of development, with different levels of mental or physical functioning, might benefit from the support of a clinical psychologist. In subsequent chapters we outline the theories and methods that clinical psychologists apply in their attempts to help the people they work with.

Chapter 3
Tools of the trade

Clinical psychologists have a set of competencies, rather like tools in a toolbox, which they learn during training, and then develop further throughout their professional careers. This toolbox includes assessment, formulation, intervention, research and evaluation, consultation, supervision, teaching/education, and leadership/management. Depending on the task, clinical psychologists might use these tools directly, for example when working as therapists; or indirectly, when working as educators, researchers, managers, or supervisors. Although none of these competencies are unique to clinical psychologists per se, it is the systematic and in-depth use of this comprehensive set of competencies, which characterizes clinical psychology.

Assessment

The first key competence is to thoroughly assess the problem or challenge that the client brings. Not surprisingly it makes sense to spend time finding out exactly what the issue is before starting to try to address it. We must also consider whether a problem needs addressing right now, and if so, what kind of support might be most appropriate, and who may be in the best position to provide this. Some difficulties may simply resolve with time and it isn't always helpful to bring in the professionals. For example, parents may seek help for a child who appears very clingy and demanding, but the assessment may suggest this is a reaction to recent family changes (such as moving to a new city), and will likely reduce as the family settles down. So there is probably no need for immediate input, even though the parents may naturally feel worried for a while.

Research has also shown that for many people, it isn't advisable to provide psychological therapy immediately following a traumatic event, since attempts to intervene professionally in the early days after trauma are actually counterproductive and may hamper the natural recovery process. For most people (and communities), the normal, although distressing, responses to trauma will slowly subside: only a relatively small minority will at some point need in-depth psychological help.

What a psychological assessment is like

There are a number of different methods that can be used to assess clients' difficulties including interviews, observation, *psychometric* or *personality measures* (like rating scales or questionnaires), administration of *test batteries* (a series of formally administered tasks which examine certain psychological functions), and gathering information from family, colleagues, or treatment notes.

If you were to attend an initial assessment, you would immediately notice the clinical psychologist making considerable efforts to put you at ease and to understand what has led you to seek or to be referred for psychological help. Most people feel anxious about being assessed by professionals and may be reluctant to talk openly about what is bothering them unless they feel sure that the professional is trustworthy and sympathetic. Normally the clinical psychologist would ask about your main concerns and difficulties, how you feel, and how easy you find it to think psychologically about things. They will also ask about the origins, development, and consequences of your concerns, how you have coped so far, any related health problems or previous treatments (including medication), and what you hope to get from coming. In addition, the psychologist would try to understand what else is going on in your life, what your family and social situation is like, and whether there are others whose views could appropriately shed light on the issue.

The initial meeting is likely to be quite wide ranging, although this of course depends on who or what is being assessed. Many assessments include close observation: if, for example, a parent seeks help for a very shy child, the clinical psychologist will want to see how both parent and child respond to the new situation of meeting a stranger (the clinical psychologist) for the first time. The clinical psychologist will also monitor their own personal reactions: do they feel uneasy, protective, or flattered, for example? Such feelings may in some cases reveal important aspects of the client's personality and relationship style. Sometimes the clinical psychologist will want to observe the client in the place where the difficulty most often occurs, like in school or hospital. Or they might ask clients to keep records, for example about their thoughts or typical daily activities.

During this first meeting, the clinical psychologist usually checks the client actively consents to being seen, and will also provide information about confidentiality, and the limits to this. Normally this means explaining that although details of what is said are not routinely shared with others, results of some tests and general information about progress and themes covered will be communicated to the doctor or team making the referral. The clinical psychologist will also explain that their 'duty of care' to the client and society as a whole is to pass on anything which suggests there might be a serious risk to the client or someone else, particularly a child. Finally the clinical psychologist will assess risk: is the client in danger of harm, or of committing any harmful acts to themselves or others? If so, this would require immediate action like providing a list of resources, alerting medical services, or even notifying the police. In such cases, the clinical psychologist might advise that this would probably not be a good time for psychological intervention. Risk needs to be reduced to a manageable level first, especially as we know that some interventions can trigger difficult emotions or behaviour.

Many clinical psychologists use psychometric tools to provide additional information. These usually take the form of simple paper and pencil, or computerized questionnaires, which ask the person about their experiences, thoughts, and emotions. These let the clinical psychologist compare the client's scores with scores from other people who are otherwise similar. There is no right or wrong ways of answering; responses just give an indication of the person's own experience. Examples include checklists of types of thoughts common in mental health problems, like 'I often feel weepy'; or 'I need to keep reassuring myself that I have locked the front door'. Other measures concern behaviours, as might be found for instance amongst children who are having difficulties: 'My son finds it impossible to control his temper'.

Given that all of us sometimes feel weepy, or from time to time return and check things, or lose our tempers, the test must be sensitive enough to spot when a profile is significantly different, and also to demonstrate what is known as *validity* and *reliability*. Put simply, 'validity' means that the measure consists of questions that can clearly distinguish people who are experiencing anxiety (for instance) from people who are experiencing something else (like depression), while 'reliability' means that the measure gives consistent results over time.

Some clinical psychologists also administer tests which aim to classify someone's personality. These ask the person about their typical behaviour or feelings, for example: 'I enjoy meeting new people'; or to describe their child's personality: 'He often needs reassurance from others'. The problem with all these tests of course is that answers can be easily influenced by what the person wants the clinical psychologist to think, or feels they ought to say (known as *demand characteristics*). One alternative assessment tool is the projective test. Here the clinical psychologist gives the client an ambiguous picture, say of an inkblot or of a small family grouping, and asks the client to describe what they see. The idea here is that the client perceives something salient to them in the ambiguous picture, thereby providing useful information about their unconscious thoughts and feelings. This type of assessment is however susceptible to the clinical psychologist's own biases and projections, and is not frequently used nowadays, being deemed less scientific than other personality measures.

In some cases assessment may consist of a test battery (mentioned earlier), which examines certain psychological functions, like speed of cognitive processing (thinking) or verbal fluency. Such functions are known to vary significantly between people and can also be affected by any damage or injury to the brain. These tests examine (for instance) a person's ability to name objects, recognize shapes, or manipulate figures within a certain time frame. Sometimes these tests result in specific scores used to categorize people, such as 'has high verbal intelligence', 'of average overall IQ', or 'intellectually disabled'.

In other cases the clinical psychologist examines the pattern of test results to see if a certain pattern of scores is suggestive of brain injury or changes to the brain (see the clinical example in Box 14). Again the clinical psychologist will usually compare the person's results with those of others to see whether there is an unusual or dysfunctional response pattern. Comparing the person's scores today with those they obtained previously allows the clinical psychologist to see if there have been changes, perhaps due to treatment or because of deterioration of an underlying condition.

Although all psychological therapies or interventions are preceded by assessment, not all assessments lead to further work. In some cases (e.g. where the purpose is to investigate the possibility of

Box 14 Paul, injured after being out drinking, is assessed by a clinical psychologist

Paul, a young man who had fallen down a steep flight of stone steps after being out drinking, sustained a serious head injury and a broken arm. Paul was discharged from hospital after a couple of days. Although Paul reported feeling physically okay, his girlfriend noticed that he had not been himself since the accident; that he had been much more quick-tempered and thoughtless about others. A clinical psychologist then met Paul to assess the impact of his head injury on his cognitive functioning. In fact this was not the first time Paul had sustained an injury after being out drinking, so the clinical psychologist was able to compare scores from a number of tests given on previous occasions. The results indicated deterioration, so Paul was re-referred to neurologists in the hospital for further medical investigations.

brain damage or the outcome of a ward treatment programme), the assessment process is the sole focus of meeting and may be a one-off, or it may take several sessions. The outcome is then communicated to the team, who will take the next steps. And although it is always the first step for psychological intervention, from therapy to organizational change initiatives, assessment doesn't stop when the intervention starts. Any understanding is always provisional, to be confirmed or disconfirmed as time progresses and as new information emerges. For example, assessments may need to be repeated as children grow and develop, and circumstances in school and home life change.

Finally, of course, assessment works both ways. It is not only the clinical psychologist who assesses the client's needs and suitability for psychological work, but clients also assess what it might be like to consult a clinical psychologist, and whether they can imagine themselves working well with this particular person.

Formulation

The second key competence, the formulation, is the vital (although often invisible) step that occurs between assessment and intervention (i.e. doing something about the difficulty that led someone to ask for help). Although there are some parallels with diagnosis in medicine, the difference between the two is that diagnosis seeks to place a person within a pre-existing illness category, while formulation aims to develop a model of each unique individual or situation within a specific social context. In practice the two processes often work together, and clinical psychologists may also use diagnostic categories like 'PTSD' or 'autism' as shorthand, as part of their wider formulation.

Formulation is also a key component of the reflective scientist-practitioner approach outlined in Chapter 1. The starting point is the information gained from the assessment, but added to this are ideas from theory which seek to explain why people behave and feel as they do, plus evidence from research. Together these lead to a speculative understanding of why this person (or family or team) has this particular difficulty at this particular time, and furthermore, what can be done which evidence suggests should (hopefully) improve things in the future. Importantly, a formulation can never be totally accurate or comprehensive. It is a set of working hypotheses that may change over time when new information emerges about the clients' experiences, their context, and their response to any specific psychological interventions. Although any given formulation is never 'true' or perfect, having a framework is important for both psychologist and client. In many respects formulation is the cornerstone of the clinical psychologist's job.

The precise nature of the formulation depends on the theoretical framework chosen (see Chapter 4). One common way of formulating, often used in cognitive behaviour therapy (CBT), is the *5 P's model* that identifies and links the Predisposing, Precipitating, Presenting, Perpetuating, and Protective factors in a person's difficulties or situation. This is normally presented as a tailor-made diagram for each client, and shared as part of the intervention. See Figure 2 for an example of such a diagrammatic formulation of a client suffering from extreme perfectionism.

By contrast, psychodynamic therapists focus on re-enactments of emotions from the past in the present therapeutic relationship. Essentially a psychodynamic formulation is a hypothesized account of patterns in relationships resulting in distress, drawing links between: (i) the current life situation; (ii) early infantile relations; and (iii) the relationship with the therapist. The psychodynamic psychotherapist won't actively share a diagram of their formulation with their client; rather they will share small parts of the formulation verbally, testing them out by observing the client's response and making interpretations.

Yet another approach to formulation is for both therapist and client to construct an agreed 'story' or narrative, either written or spoken, detailing and explaining the person's current predicaments and distress, and suggesting how things might be changed in future.

No matter what type of formulation is used, it works best when it demonstrates an empathic understanding of the client's difficulties, their origin, maintenance, and consequences, in ways that ring true and allow the possibility of hope and positive change.

Intervention

The third competence is intervention. Here the clinical psychologist chooses an approach, technique, or therapy, aimed at assisting the client, and then implements this in collaboration

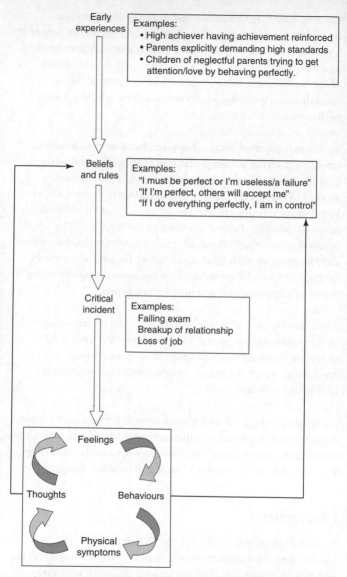

Early
experiences

Examples:
• High achiever having achievement reinforced
• Parents explicitly demanding high standards
• Children of neglectful parents trying to get
  attention/love by behaving perfectly.

Beliefs
and rules

Examples:
"I must be perfect or I'm useless/a failure"
"If I'm perfect, others will accept me"
"If I do everything perfectly, I am in control"

Critical
incident

Examples:
Failing exam
Breakup of relationship
Loss of job

Feelings

Thoughts   Behaviours

Physical
symptoms

Clinical Psychology

2. A diagrammatic formulation of a client suffering from extreme
perfectionism.

with the client. The key skill is translating science into clinical practice: being able to apply knowledge of evidence and a wide range of theoretical frameworks to solve current clinical concerns.

The choice of intervention is guided by the formulation and the client's preference, and could include a huge array of things, ranging from individual psychotherapy to access to telephone support, establishing staff training events, modifying a ward treatment plan, or attending therapeutic meetings with a group of people with similar problems. Interventions may take place on a one-to-one basis or involve others, for instance staff in a care home, family members, or schoolteachers.

Interventions may also be short-term or take several years, although within public service settings, there is considerable pressure to deliver brief, cost-effective interventions. For instance, the NHS in the UK mostly uses a tiered system of provision for people needing psychological therapy. The initial step is guided self-help, such as computerized therapy or self-help books.

If the person doesn't improve, they may then be offered second-tier services: a limited number of sessions of individual or group therapy, often using a manualized treatment format (procedures written down and specified in advance). These may be provided by a therapist trained in a specific type of therapy such as CBT (see Chapter 4), and supervised by a clinical psychologist. Indeed clinical psychologists are often involved in designing, setting up, and evaluating these first two tiers of services, which have been shown to be effective for many people. Some clients will however need more intensive therapy, so there is a third tier of services, usually one-to-one. The therapies offered here often use more individualized formulations, although most are still based within one or more of the therapeutic models, such as CBT.

There are numerous variations around this way of working, with some clinical psychologists offering much longer or shorter therapies. Nevertheless, a typical course of more intensive psychological therapy for adults comprises a series of weekly or fortnightly appointments of about an hour each, lasting between six and thirty weeks. The format differs for work with children, which often involves play or drawing. The focus is on the client's concerns, with minimal preliminary social conversation. There is no physical contact between participants beyond possibly a handshake. The clinical psychologist sometimes takes notes, although this may be done after the session. The client does most of the talking about their experiences and feelings, with the clinical psychologist actively involved, asking questions, suggesting alternative ways of seeing the issue, or developing plans to help the client change things in the future.

Evaluation

Following a particular intervention, it is important to evaluate whether it was effective or not. This is done by observing the client's response, measuring symptom change, and/or asking the client for feedback. Essentially, evaluation involves being curious about what occurred as a result of some action, and collecting enough data to be able to reach conclusions about its impact. This knowledge then allows clinical psychologists to make changes for the future. In routine clinical practice this is normally done by simply asking the client or family if the situation has improved and why, and also by repeating any tests given before the intervention to see if there is a difference afterwards. The majority of clinical psychologists regularly evaluate their work and involve their clients in doing so. Some services ask clients to provide feedback after every session, which can act as early warning signs that the current intervention is not helping and that a different approach may be needed.

Research and audit

Although there are always time pressures, many clinical psychologists conduct more complicated forms of evaluation such as small-scale audits. These involve examination of sets of data collected by particular practices or services. Results from these audits are fed directly back into practice, thus ensuring that more effective services continue to be funded, replacing less effective services.

Some clinical psychologists also participate in research, often collaborating with local academic institutions. This normally entails the systematic investigation of some clinical phenomena or treatment using a broad range of measures, points of observation, types of outcome, and forms of analysis. Research can help to develop a better understanding of some clinical condition (e.g. autism), or to evaluate the effects of a particular type of therapy (e.g. could IPT be useful to help teenagers who abuse alcohol?), or to understand the effective processes in therapy (like the quality of relationship between the psychologist and client) and their effect on therapy outcome.

Such studies also help develop theoretical understanding about human functioning, especially when people are distressed. This research contributes to the development of clinical psychology as an applied discipline, and hence will help those who may consult clinical psychologists in the future. Many research-active clinical psychologists also try to increase the impact of their research or audits by sharing the results through publication in academic journals, by writing books and by presenting papers at conferences.

Consultation, teaching, supervision, management and leadership

We have mostly focused in this chapter on work with individual clients but clinical psychologists also work with organizations, by providing advice and consultancy (e.g. on how best to establish team working) and by providing teaching/education for staff. Supervision forms a key part of the training and ongoing practice of many professional groups in health and social care, and clinical psychologists increasingly contribute to this, both by conducting research on how to supervise most effectively and by providing supervision directly. Key components include setting up formal supervision contracts, and paying careful attention to the quality of the relationship between supervisor and supervisee.

Many clinical psychologists also take on management and leadership roles. They may be involved as clinical leaders, encouraging colleagues to take account of psychological perspectives (through providing supervision and information), or they may have roles as organizational advisors and managers. With their specialized training in communication skills and a culture of taking on board others' perspective, clinical psychologists can make a valuable contribution to leadership in the organizations in which they work (e.g. participating in meetings, administration, and formal policy-setting).

This chapter has given you a look at what's inside the clinical psychologist's toolbox, including assessment, formulation, intervention, research and evaluation, consultation, supervision, teaching/education, and leadership/management. In the following chapter we look at how the formulation leads to action, and the ways that clinical psychologists have used theories to help them decide on what to do next.

Chapter 4
Frameworks used by clinical psychologists

In this chapter, we turn to the theoretical ideas and concepts that underpin the application of the competencies outlined in Chapter 3. All professionals rely on the use of frameworks (models and theories) to understand and help their clients. These frameworks provide structure and practical guidance as to what needs to be done next. Clinical psychologists are trained to apply a number of different psychological frameworks in their work, which function a bit like maps in an unknown terrain. These maps indicate what is most likely to be going on and may be causing difficulties, and also provide guidance as to what can be done to help.

First: a word of caution. Theoretical frameworks are important to psychologists in suggesting how to understand their clients and to structure interventions. However, as long as there is a conceptual framework that both the therapist and client believe in, exactly which particular framework is used is less important to clients. In fact, research shows that from the viewpoint of the person receiving therapy, the most important thing is having help from someone who is kind, thoughtful, respectful, and hopeful, and who has a shared understanding of the problem at hand, together with a clear plan of how to address it.

Many studies have found that having a good therapeutic relationship between client and therapist, and the client's willingness to make changes, are better predictors of outcome than any specific framework or technique. The clinical psychologist will use a particular framework depending on the service context, client preferences, research evidence, clinical guidelines, and their own judgement. We'll now look at some specific examples of frameworks, and when they might be helpful and applicable.

Behavioural frameworks

From the early days of the profession, clinical psychologists started to apply the principles of learning (such as conditioning, behavioural modification, rewards, and shaping) to improve peoples' mental health (these principles are discussed in more detail in Butler and McManus's VSI, *Psychology*). For example, in the 1960s and 1970s clinical psychologists set up 'token economies' within the old mental hospitals, which established new rules and innovative ways of rewarding previously institutionalized inmates. Staff members in these communities were trained to give tokens as rewards, which could be exchanged for goods or privileges, to patients for joining in social activities and learning new skills, thus stimulating patients to move progressively towards more independent living. This work was based on behavioural modification principles known as 'selective reinforcement' and 'shaping'.

Such behavioural principles underpin the techniques and practices of behaviour therapy, which was (and still is) used in treating many mental health difficulties, including phobias and anxiety. Understanding exactly how people learn things (including fear) showed psychologists how avoiding something that makes someone anxious can be paradoxically rewarding in itself, because of the relief the person feels when the thing is avoided. This can then unhelpfully maintain their fear (see the clinical examples in Box 15).

Box 15 Barbara and Abdul each get help from clinical psychologists for their phobias

Barbara had always been afraid of dogs. When she recently moved to the suburbs, this fear worsened, since in order to get to work, Barbara had to cross a park where residents often walked their dogs. She tried to avoid the dogs by going to work very early and coming back very late in the day or by taking a much longer route to work. The clinical psychologist set up a programme whereby Barbara agreed first to observe the psychologist approaching and stroking a small dog; then to approach a small dog herself; then to accompany the psychologist when approaching larger dogs; and then to pat a small dog herself. Eventually, to her great delight (and warm congratulations from her psychologist), Barbara could cheerfully cross the park on her own and greet dogs that would approach her. Although she remained 'not a big fan of dogs', Barbara was able to get to and from work without feeling overwhelmed with anxiety.

While serving in the forces, Abdul had been involved in hostilities and, after becoming a civilian, had grown intolerant of noise, leading him to withdraw from most social situations, staying home with his family. A behavioural programme involving Abdul's family helped Abdul to gradually increase his frequency in going out to noisy places, with his much-loved niece offering to spend more time with him, as a 'reward', only when he went out. This helped Abdul to habituate to noise, learning that doing so was not actually harmful and also that avoidance was not as much fun as going out.

Behaviour therapy has been applied in numerous other ways, for instance in developing social behaviour or language in children with intellectual disability, or in designing programmes to help people with acquired brain injury to re-learn behaviours like how to dress or feed themselves again. Some clinical psychologists provide teaching or supervision for other groups of professional staff on using these techniques. For example many community nurses now use the principles of behaviour therapy and reinforcement to help families to toilet-train young children or to develop their healthy eating habits; while some secure hospital staff apply behavioural programmes to help offenders develop improved anger control.

Cognitive frameworks

Despite its successes, the limits to behaviour therapy soon became apparent, particularly because it had neglected cognition. Cognition is the process by which people make sense of the world through perceiving, thinking, storing, and applying information, and by using language, including how we use our senses, remember, forget, organize, and structure what we have learned. So clinical psychologists started drawing upon cognitive frameworks to enable them to better understand and help people.

Academic studies have shown that our senses don't simply pass signals neutrally in and out of our brains, but that an enormous amount of internal processing goes on, much of it affected by the limitations and constraints of memory, past experience, expectation, mood, and motivation. Psychologists have suggested that in some ways we resemble computers, and function by constructing, elaborating, and applying a variety of sense-making 'programmes' known as *schema* (or ways of understanding events). But although we have an enormous potential to learn and understand things, our schema are nevertheless also rather faulty, limited, and biased. In fact our schema are reliant on short cuts, stored assumptions, and socially or culturally acquired constructions. So in fact we don't process things neutrally like a computer might, but interpret them, often semi-automatically—despite also being highly efficient learners who can also take charge and control much of what happens, at least on a conscious level.

Since we operate *psycho*logically, not logically, we are therefore sometimes subject to making a number of thinking errors. These include jumping to conclusions, over-generalizing, black-and-white thinking, and catastrophic thinking (e.g. deciding everything is forever hopeless based on one bad thing happening). Significantly, there appear to be differences between people in exactly how these processes work. Research suggests that our individual schema depend to some extent on our life experiences, unique histories, social contexts, biology, and personal dispositions.

Such ideas from cognitive psychology have been progressively applied within clinical psychology, resulting in cognitive therapy. The idea is that many of the schema held by distressed people play a central role in much of their emotional suffering. Some people in some circumstances appear to be particularly prone to making errors of judgement, and may therefore tend to see neutral but ambiguous events as negative or hostile. This then confirms their negative thinking, leading to a downward spiral. Imagine for example that I am expecting my friend to telephone me for a chat to cheer me up following a disappointment over a job interview. When she doesn't call, there are a number of possible explanations: she has lost my phone number, she had to go urgently to visit a sick relative, she forgot to call, she has lost her mobile phone, or she does not like me anymore. Given that I am already feeling disappointed, I may well decide her dislike for me is the reason. I am of course even more likely to reach this conclusion if many of my past experiences have led me to expect similar rejections from others. Thinking this then unfortunately leads me to feel even worse.

A key notion is that how we think about ourselves determines our experience: a famous quote from Epictetus from over 2000 years ago is: 'men are disturbed not by things but by the views which they take of them'. In other words, there is a close link between thoughts and emotion, so that negative thoughts can actually *cause* negative emotions. It is the thought that my friend does not like me that causes my mood to drop.

Cognitive therapy was first introduced for people with depression, but it is now used with a wide range of problems, including anxiety, post-traumatic stress disorder, eating difficulties, and psychosis. In all these cases, clinical psychologists attend closely to how people think, and how their thoughts and beliefs may inadvertently cause or worsen their emotional distress. The clinical psychologist works with the client to reveal and check the assumptions and evidence that underpin their thoughts. These procedures are referred to as *Socratic questioning* (seeking to get the client to answer their own questions by making them think, and drawing out the answer from the client, rather than telling them the answer), and *thought challenging* (encouraging the client to test out their assumptions, for example asking: 'Are there any other possible explanations you can think of?'). The development of specific cognitive models for understanding particular types of distress has been particularly important, and has also encouraged research into the most effective ways of helping a wide range of clients.

Cognitive behaviour therapy (CBT) draws upon both cognitive and behavioural frameworks, using cognitive techniques like Socratic questioning and thought challenging, together with techniques developed in behaviour therapy, like the systematic use of reinforcement and shaping (see Box 16 for a clinical example). Other techniques include using guided experimentation, sometimes known as *behavioural experiments*. (See Figure 3 for an example of a behavioural experiment set up for a client with a fear of public speaking.) CBT is mainly focused on reducing symptoms and often involves exercises or homework to be completed by the client between sessions.

CBT has been taken up enthusiastically in clinical psychology, and has been shown to be effective for many conditions, supported by

Box 16 A clinical psychologist helps a teenager who struggles in social situations

Pavel, a teenage schoolboy, was anxious about meeting others, often retreating from social gatherings outside school. His clinical psychologist used Socratic questioning (seeking to get the client to answer their own questions by making them think and drawing out the answer from them) to discover what Pavel was thinking as peers approached him. Pavel replied: 'They are all so confident, they can see how boring I am, they can see me blushing, they are judging me, they don't like me'. The clinical psychologist agreed that being nervous would be entirely understandable if those assumptions (cognitions) were accurate, but then asked Pavel to explore whether those assumptions were in fact true. He asked Pavel to conduct tests (behavioural experiments) such as doing a survey at school about how others also feel at the start of social events. The results of the survey helped Pavel appreciate that others are often anxious too, and wouldn't be focusing on his blushes. This then gave Pavel more confidence to respond more positively when others approached him socially.

numerous research studies. Many of the examples elsewhere in this VSI make reference to the use of CBT by clinical psychologists.

Psychodynamic frameworks

Originally developed by Freud in the last part of the 19th century, psychodynamic theories were in the past highly influential within many mental health professions, including clinical psychology. Over the years, however, many of the ideas and practices have altered significantly, so very few clinical psychologists today would apply traditional Freudian notions such as asking clients to lie on

Behavioural Experiment

Prediction
What is your prediction?
What do you expect will happen?
How would you know if it came true?

If I speak in public I will shake so much that people will notice and laugh at me

Rate how strongly you believe this will happen (0-100%)

90%

Experiment
What experiment could test this prediction? (where & when)
What safety behaviours will need to be dropped?
How would you know your prediction had come true?

Speak up at the next meeting on Monday - I could present some of the data that I have been meaning to show.
Would need to gesture with my hands, and not hold on to the table
I could ask my friends if they noticed me shaking when I talk

Outcome
What happened?
Was your prediction accurate?

I was really nervous and was very aware of my hands
My friends said I spoke well and that they could not see me shake

Learning
What did you learn?
How likely is it that your predictions will happen in the future?

Although I feel nervous when speaking it's not as obvious to other people

Rate how strongly you agree with your original prediction now (0-100%)

50%

3. An example of a behavioural experiment worksheet.

a couch or using dream interpretation. Nevertheless, many other psychodynamic ideas are still respected, and research has also supported the efficacy of many psychodynamically oriented approaches, especially brief, focused psychotherapy, which aims to help people improve their interpersonal relationships. Many clinical psychologists working in private practice use therapies that are based on psychodynamic ideas.

Key psychodynamic concepts include the importance of intimate personal relationships for healthy psychological development, and our need as humans to feel love and be loved. More recently this has been understood in terms of our need for attachment to others, a process which is both biologically and psychologically crucial for survival. Clinical psychologists have shown that if there are distortions in early attachments (e.g. when parents are unavailable to the child, say through illness, abuse, or abandonment), this can lead to significant distortions in personality development and later psychological problems.

Another important concept is that of defence mechanisms, whereby we try to protect ourselves from uncomfortable feelings. For example, we can be dismayingly unaware of undesirable traits in ourselves, and quick to attribute them to others instead (*projection*). We can mask an attitude by emphasizing its opposite, like the anti-pornography crusader who reveals his own fascination with pornography by finding pornographic material to protest about (*reaction formation*). We can direct our feelings towards the wrong person, like the woman who feels angry with her boss, but when returning home, starts a fight with her husband or kicks the cat (*displacement*). Or we can disclaim responsibility for our behaviour by attributing it to circumstances beyond our control (*externalization*). We are infinitely creative in finding ways to avoid or disavow what is distressing or threatening!

Another of Freud's key observations was that when in therapy, people tend to repeat, with the therapist, some significant aspects of their early relationships. That is, they may relate to their therapist in the present (as a neutral authority figure), rather like they used to relate to authority figures (such as parents) in the past. This is known as *transference*. In therapy, therapists aim to interpret both transference and defence mechanisms so that the client is able to understand (gain insight) into these, and thereby develop healthier relationship patterns in the present. For example, a therapist might say to a client something like 'When you turned to your father for help, he humiliated you. Given what you've experienced, it's not surprising that you now expect the same treatment from me.'

Systemic frameworks

None of us exist in isolation. Or as nicely stated by John Donne: 'No man is an island, entire unto himself'. To some extent we are all part of families, communities, schools, organizations, and the wider society. Systemic theories propose that our personal experience of psychological distress has a lot to do with how we relate to others, and how they relate to us. Wider social forces may also play a big part, shown by the impact of experiences like poverty, stereotyping, or racial prejudice on people's mental health. Evidence shows that mental health worsens in times of economic austerity, and it is quite clear that inequality in society significantly adds to levels of psychological distress.

Systemic theories focus on the influence that people and the organizations that surround us have in shaping our sense of identity, relationships, behaviour, and beliefs. Rather than trying to encourage change in an individual with a problem, systemically based therapies aim to change systems, that is, to alter how people relate to one another. Someone with difficult behaviour may be understood as a symptom or sign of difficulties in society or the family, not simply as an isolated problem.

So an intervention would be offered to the family, school, or community, not just the individual person, with the aim of changing the underlying dynamic.

For example, family therapy might be provided for the whole family where, say, a 'difficult' older woman is refusing to move into sheltered accommodation despite her family's wishes. Working systemically, the psychologist may help the family to see things from the older woman's viewpoint, and that her agitation has resulted in part from her sense of being controlled by her family. The family's concerns would also be explored, and it might transpire that they have a number of other serious problems (e.g. relating to finance or housing). This then might require involvement by social services, besides help from the team directly providing psychological care for the older woman.

Family therapy has also been shown to help people with serious mental health problems, by helping their families to cope better with the demands of living with someone whose behaviour may be unstable and unpredictable. Or family members might not be aware of how they are colluding with avoidance of certain feelings or behaviours, or reinforcing the problematic behaviour (e.g. a mother helping her son to perform complicated cleaning rituals, even though she doesn't feel the need to do so herself). Finally, clinical psychologists working in organizations such as care homes or hospital wards may use systemic approaches (as well as behavioural techniques) to try and change environments that inadvertently encourage unwanted behaviour in their residents or clients, such as aggression, passivity, or dependence (see the example of Ramon in Chapter 2).

Integrative frameworks

Given their training in a number of frameworks, in practice many clinical psychologists use a combination of theoretical techniques and ideas to suit the person in front of them. Box 17 describes

Box 17 A clinical psychologist helps a young boy and his foster family

Ryan and Judy had been providing foster care for 5-year-old Tom for about ten months and had become concerned about his behaviour. Although initially he had been charming and easy to care for, over the last few months Tom's behaviour at home had significantly deteriorated (shouting, swearing, rudeness). He was however behaving well at school, which he evidently enjoyed. Ryan and Judy were particularly worried about Tom's abusive language and disobedience towards Judy—this happened much less towards Ryan. They felt that things might improve if the family service gave Tom psychotherapy for the early abuse and neglect that he had suffered prior to being fostered.

The clinical psychologist met with Ryan and Judy, and with consent from the family, also spoke with Tom's social worker to get more information on his background. But after listening carefully to the foster parents' concerns, the clinical psychologist suggested that, although some of Tom's behaviour might be best understood in the context of his early history, it might be more helpful for the parents to make a few changes to their current management of Tom's troubling behaviour. For example, Ryan could explicitly model appropriate ways of behaving towards Judy, and talk to Tom about this.

The clinical psychologist also recommended that together they attend a group for foster carers on ways of building attachment, explaining that bringing in an outside expert therapist to work directly with Tom at this stage might further undermine Judy's authority, and could interfere with the development of healthy respect and attachment between Judy and Tom. Although Ryan was unable to attend the suggested support group, Judy was able to do so, and successfully introduced some new strategies to improve relationships in the family, like having shared mealtimes. At a follow-up meeting a few weeks later, both foster carers reported substantial improvement in Tom's behaviour and his relationship with Judy.

how a clinical psychologist might do this by offering a personalized intervention specifically for the needs of a particular client and his family.

In recent years a number of integrative therapy approaches have been developed which systematically combine and integrate key elements of other frameworks or ideas. For example psychologists have incorporated some ideas from Eastern philosophy into cognitive therapy, leading to mindfulness-based cognitive therapy (MBCT), which includes meditation and mindfulness practice. The aim of MBCT is to reduce people's ever-active thought processes, which MBCT proposes simply encourage anxiety and can fuel people's relentless, unfulfillable desires. MBCT teaches clients that their thoughts (including anxieties, ruminations, and judgements) are simply thoughts, which only have power because people choose to attend to them and try to change them. People would be happier if they could learn simply to accept and observe their thoughts, letting them go (i.e. not getting stuck on thoughts about the past or the future) and living more fully in the present.

Another integrative example is acceptance and commitment therapy (ACT), which combines acceptance and mindfulness principles with behaviour-change strategies, in order to increase psychological flexibility (see Box 18 for a clinical example). ACT proposes that rather than trying to eliminate or control difficult feelings and thoughts (like CBT) we should just 'notice' and learn not to act upon them. And instead of avoiding situations where they are invoked, we should 'move towards' our values (what is most important to our true selves), and commit to action (setting goals according to our values).

A final example is cognitive analytic therapy (CAT), popular in the UK. This combines cognitive/behavioural approaches, psychodynamic thinking, and systemic ideas. The key proposal is that we are best understood in terms of patterns of relationships and reciprocated behaviours, which are developed early and tend

Box 18 A clinical example of infertility and how a clinical psychologist might be helpful

Bianca had managed the stress of several failed in vitro fertilization (IVF) attempts reasonably well, although over the last year things had been particularly difficult. In addition to the financial burden, Bianca's sister-in-law had given birth, and Bianca found it increasingly distressing to visit her sister-in-law or to see friends with young children. Her stress and anger about the infertility began to escalate, putting a strain on Bianca and Aaron's relationship. The couple described their lives as dominated by infertility and the need to put their life 'on hold'. Aaron reported that their sexual relationship, once passionate and spontaneous, was now replaced with timed intercourse, stress, and pressure.

Using ACT principles, the psychologist helped the couple gradually to accept and come to terms with feelings of disappointment, failure, and inadequacy. This entailed helping them to reduce their judgemental thoughts and evaluations about their inability to conceive by learning to simply observe their critical thoughts, thus decreasing their believability. At first, Bianca in particular struggled with the concept of acceptance; over time however she learned that acceptance of distress did not imply giving up on her journey toward parenthood, but helped her to think and to feel emotions without avoidance. Also, clarifying what they valued about parenthood allowed the couple to explore options, from continued treatments to adoption or using a gestational carrier.

to recur across many current situations. Sometimes these patterns are helpful to us (e.g. I act kindly to you when you are sad, like my mother did to me, and I am also kind to myself when I am sad), but sometimes they are unhelpful (e.g. I ridicule you when you are sad, like I was ridiculed as a child, and I also condemn myself when I am sad).

Box 19 A clinical psychologist helps Lizzy to relate to people in new ways

Lizzy told her therapist that, as a child, she had always felt inferior. She described feeling frightened but also resentful of her vivacious but emotionally unstable actress mother, whom Lizzy felt she had to placate in order to be loved. Lizzy's clinical psychologist noted that Lizzy's romantic life included a series of failed relationships, where she put her own needs second to that of her partner, resulting in regular stormy outbreaks where she would express her deep anger at being taken for granted, followed by weepy apologies and attempts to make up again by abasing herself. In addition the clinical psychologist observed that Lizzy would attempt to do and say the 'right' thing in therapy sessions but would then express resentment, and on occasions, fail to attend appointments. Therapy involved discovering and tracing these patterns, and trying to establish new ways of relating both in the relationship with the therapist, and in the world outside therapy.

CAT sees distress as resulting from our early attempts to deal with difficulties, which might have worked previously, but are now ineffectual or harmful. These attempts nevertheless become habitual patterns, which are really hard to shift. The clinical psychologist and the client collaboratively formulate these patterns, and explore how the client could develop alternative, healthier patterns. Sometimes this may involve trying out new ways of relating to the therapist within the safe confines of the professional relationship (see the clinical example in Box 19).

This chapter has outlined the major frameworks and therapy approaches used by clinical psychologists in their daily practice. We now turn to an examination of what it is actually like to be a clinical psychologist, and what challenges and triumphs clinical psychologists may regularly experience when at work.

Chapter 5
Developing our identity as reflective scientist-practitioners

What on earth would motivate someone to spend their entire working lives listening to unhappy stories or trying to make sense of the internal conflicts of others, rather than, say, maximizing profit for a company, teaching children to swim, or designing fashionable clothes or buildings?

Most clinical psychologists respond that they have a deep seated desire to help other people (especially the disadvantaged or marginalized) to lead more fulfilled lives, together with a wish to understand diversity and a determination to make a difference in life. Most would add that they have a strong sense of curiosity, are fascinated by the human psyche, and want to gain a better understanding of human behaviour and emotions. There are so many questions: why do people feel as they do? Why do some people seem to keep repeating behaviours that make them unhappy? How can we best help troubled children? What can be done to help survivors of trauma or abuse? Why do some people appear to be starving or drinking themselves to death, and what can we do to help them to develop a healthier way of dealing with whatever is troubling them?

Other clinical psychologists might talk about how much they enjoy the intellectual challenge of responding to the complexity of people; of exploring different layers, meanings, and reasons for living with multiple challenges, multifaceted experiences, and complicated motivations. One of our supervisors once said that he was in love with his work because of its complexity. He described it as 'a constant puzzle without a one-fits-all answer or unequivocal solution'.

Some psychologists naturally enjoy listening to stories and problems, gaining satisfaction from being able to hear about people's personal experiences. They value really getting close to others, forming intimate trusting relationships, and learning to respect and value other people's unique perspectives on life. Certainly, being allowed into people's personal lives is a real honour. From our own experience, it feels an immense privilege when people trust you: when they let you in and share their vulnerable sides with you, including what they fear are shameful parts of themselves. Further, it can be inspiring to learn about the courage and resilience of many clients, especially when they are facing or have survived great trauma and hardship in their lives.

By contrast, some people develop an interest in clinical psychology through their own personal experiences, having been confronted with mental illness or psychological problems within their own families, and having had to make sense of a confusing world from early on. Others become passionate about the profession after being a client in therapy or as a result of some other personal difficulties. Or an initial interest might have been triggered by a wish to understand themselves better or the people close to them.

Many clinical psychologists further emphasize the role's variation and diversity, and how stimulating and exciting it is to integrate science, theory, and clinical practice within one profession. The interchange between establishing closeness with clients on one hand and drawing on insights from science and theory on the other makes every day challenging but stimulating. The many hats we wear as clinicians, researchers, teachers, supervisors, and team leaders and supervisees makes boredom almost impossible.

It must be said however that, as appealing as clinical psychology is, it isn't for everyone. If you enjoy giving people advice or information, it might be simpler to become a life coach or teacher. Also, if you primarily want to become a therapist, it might be quicker to seek training in counselling or a particular therapeutic model. If having formal status is important for you (like always being called 'doctor'), medicine might suit you better. If facts, logic, and the 'truth' are important to you, it might be better to enter law or the security services than to be confronted on a daily basis with the seemingly illogical and emotional decisions that many people make when in distress. Moreover, if you want to make money, it might be better to work in finance or law: unless you are lucky you may be living on stipends or loans until your 30s and may then work in public services with variable levels of pay and conditions. Or you may work privately, which will involve funding your own office, insurance, supervisor, and administrative support, plus the insecurity of self-employment.

On a personal level, the job can be very challenging. Clinical psychologists need to be open to reflection, introspection, and feedback from clients and colleagues, and able to tolerate difficult emotions. Partly due to their previous experiences, many clients don't express thanks, gratitude, or appreciation of your time and effort. People tend to contact clinical psychologists when they feel at their worst: overwhelmed by their feelings, in crisis, or on the verge of a relationship breakdown. Therefore, they may not be able to consider your feelings or needs. Occasionally clients can feel very angry and may express this towards you, irrespective of your actions or words.

Clearly, for most of us being a clinical psychologist is not just a job (there would be other simpler ways of earning a decent living). In many respects it is a way of life, having a deep seated desire to help others, a passion for people, curiosity about human difficulties, experiences, vulnerabilities, and differences, and satisfaction from the daily intellectual and emotional challenge of working with people in distress.

Clinical psychology training

The training and licensing of clinical psychologists varies between countries, but it always includes a combination of academic research and educational requirements and clinical experiences (see Figure 4). Training usually involves at least three years of undergraduate education in psychology, followed by time spent obtaining substantial clinical work experience with clients, and then by a three- to six-year doctoral academic programme.

Some clinical psychology training programmes in the USA lead to a PhD with a strong focus on research, and are typically housed in universities. Other US clinical psychology doctoral programmes focus more on therapy practice and result in a PsyD. These are usually based in private colleges and professional schools. Both types of programme take five years part-time and are self-funded. This means that most students take out enormous student loans often incurring $100,000 of debt or more over the course of their education.

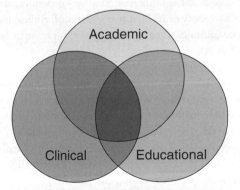

4. **The three aspects of clinical psychology training.**

In the UK, becoming a clinical psychologist requires the completion of a DClinPsych, which is a practitioner doctorate and combines clinical, academic research, and educational components. In contrast to the USA, this is normally a three-year full-time university programme, based within the NHS. The trainees are currently funded for aspects of their education and academic training while working clinically in NHS services for three or four days a week. (Note: the term 'student' is more commonly used in the USA and 'trainee' in the UK; they are used interchangeably in this VSI.)

In most Western countries, including the USA, Canada, and the UK, the practice of clinical psychology requires a licence or registration. In most countries the title 'clinical psychologist' is restricted to professionals who have successfully completed postgraduate training, are licensed in their locality, and are registered with a certain professional body. Although every country and state varies, there are usually three common requirements—a degree from an approved educational programme, a minimum amount of supervised clinical experience, and passing an examination.

Becoming a scientist

Although specific areas of interest may vary depending on the particular university or its faculty members, all clinical psychology doctoral programmes are expected to cover topics such as those shown in Box 20.

Teaching is mostly led by university faculty and supplemented by clinicians and researchers who give guest lectures. Many senior clinical psychologists continue to teach at their local universities and enjoy sharing their passion with the next generation of clinical psychologists. This way, trainees meet many local experts in the field, build professional networks, experience different approaches and styles of working, and gain insight into different services and career opportunities. Teaching formats include

Box 20 Typical academic programme of clinical psychology doctorates

- Clinical communication
- General counselling skills
- Assessment and formulation skills
- Quantitative and qualitative research methods and techniques
- Theories of psychotherapy (e.g. cognitive therapy, CBT)
- Psychopathology (e.g. personality disorders, psychosis, anxiety, depression)
- Developmental psychopathology (e.g. autism)
- Substance abuse
- Trauma, stress, and resilience
- Clinical health psychology
- Lifespan perspectives; child and adult development
- Family and child psychology
- Community psychology
- Forensic psychology
- Programme/service evaluation
- Professional ethics
- Cultural and social awareness
- Supervision, consultation, and teaching

lectures, workshops, interactive courses, and experiential learning opportunities such as role-plays and reflective groups.

As part of their academic training, trainees are continuously evaluated on their writing skills and must present numerous case reports, case conceptualizations, assessments, treatment plans, theoretical essays, literature reviews, and small-scale research projects. Doctoral programmes also require an independent innovative empirical research project or dissertation. Conducting a doctoral dissertation is time-consuming, starting with literature reviews, establishing a research question, finding a research supervisor, developing a research proposal and appropriate research design, gaining ethical approval, recruitment, data collecting, analysis, reflecting on the results, writing up the findings in a professional publishable format, and, finally, a defence of the dissertation to senior professionals within the area of expertise. These academic requirements of case reviews, essays, literature reviews, research projects, and a dissertation mean that, besides working clinically three to four days a week, and attending classes one to two days a week, most evenings and weekends are spent either reading literature, doing academic writing, or preparing for clinical work. Training is not for the faint-hearted!

Becoming a practitioner

Whether it is called a placement, practicum, or internship, all clinical psychology doctoral training programmes include supervised clinical experience. In the USA, students choose the service/client group they want to work with from a range of accredited internships, which are centrally controlled by the Association of Psychology Postdoctoral and Internship Centers (APPIC). This means students need to undertake the time-consuming process of applying for internships (including writing cover letters, resumes, interviews, etc.) and might end up not working in their preferred site. Although sometimes experienced as laborious and stressful, this however does help students to build expertise in particular areas; it promotes their knowledge and skills; and it offers valuable practice runs of application procedures (useful for job searches after qualification).

By contrast, in the UK and other European clinical psychology training programmes, internships/placements tend to be arranged by the doctoral programme, so that trainees are allocated to placements in different local services, depending on the professional needs of the service or trainee. These trainees will have little say in the location (maybe commuting long distances for several placements), client group, service, or supervisor. Although they have less choice, this arrangement minimizes the time spent on formal application procedures, and also ensures trainees acquire a wide range of clinical experiences in working with children, adults, older adults, and people with learning disabilities.

Examination and registration

All clinical psychology programmes assess their students/trainees to ensure they have attained the required professional standards and can safely provide services to the public. Some programmes use standardized formal written exams, such as the US Examination for the Professional Practice of Psychology (EPPP). These exams provide a comprehensive assessment of the candidate's knowledge, practice, and applied skills. Although the content might differ slightly in the various countries, states, and training programmes, the format usually includes a combination of verbal (interview, presentation) and written components. Nobody enjoys being examined but almost everyone agrees that some sort of gatekeeping is required in order to protect the public and to maintain standards.

Supervision: a space for professional reflection

Clinical psychologists are not just training to become scientist-practitioners, but also to be reflective scientist-practitioners. As shown in Chapter 1, being reflective includes considering the needs, wishes, and views of different clients and their families, and working out what approach would be most helpful for each individual. Although being reflective might come naturally to some, training also requires formal reflection on the integration of science into clinical practice via supervision. A supervision session normally involves two or more professionals meeting regularly for about an hour to discuss cases and concerns brought by the supervisee. Students have to participate in individual clinical supervision with senior professionals at the local university or clinical service, as well as joining regular peer supervision groups.

Supervision aims to offer an experience to the supervisee that is formative, normative, and restorative. That is, by reflecting on client work together, it promotes learning and development of clinical skills (formative); provides an opportunity to explore expected outcomes, and managerial and ethical questions related to the client work, in line with the guidelines of the particular organization (normative); and explores the emotional effects of the client work on the supervisee (restorative).

Supervision is not unique to the training years. Most clinical psychologists continue to receive supervision for their clinical and/or research work throughout their careers. The difference between supervision as a qualified clinical psychologist and as a trainee lies mainly in its frequency (trainees tend to receive more hours of supervision per number of clients). Also, during training, supervision usually includes a fourth aim: evaluation of the supervisee's competence.

At its best, supervision creates a wonderful learning environment, allowing the supervisee to gain from the expertise of a senior experienced clinician/researcher in the field, while providing a safe place to reflect, experiment with different techniques, make mistakes, and gain feedback. The supervisor-supervisee relationship can act as a parallel process of therapist-client, or parent-child relationship, revealing aspects of the therapeutic processes that may be happening in the clinical work. This parallel process was clearly described by the positive supervision experience of one of our colleagues:

> 'that sense that you could throw anything at my supervisor, and knowing that she wouldn't freak out...so building that real sense of trust'.

Hopefully this sense of safety and 'being held' was also the experience of the client in therapy.

At its worst, however, supervisees can feel criticized, judged, scrutinized, and unsafe, with supervision simply becoming a place to please the supervisor:

> It's a really difficult relationship because…it's a power relationship and she is evaluating me: She is qualified and has more power…. That's difficult with someone who you're meant to reflect with and be really open and genuine with about how you're feeling.

Personal reflection in therapy

Besides professional reflection, another part of being a reflective scientist-practitioner is personal reflection. Self-understanding matters because psychologists should not impose their own 'baggage' or personal biases and concerns onto their clients. Hence many training programmes actively encourage their trainees to undergo personal therapy as part of their professional development (see also Chapter 6). Other programmes, however, don't stress the potential benefit of personal therapy, and focus more on the trainee's professional development. Some programmes offer regular reflective or process groups where trainees and staff are expected to share personal experiences (i.e. family background, relationships), whereas others explicitly state that the staff team is respectful of boundaries between trainees' personal and professional lives, so that personal issues aren't openly shared.

The person behind the professional

Working as a clinical psychologist, with troubled clients, in stretched services, and with stressed colleagues, isn't for everyone. It never becomes easy, although you usually learn how to handle things better over the years. Some difficulties remain inherent to the role of clinical psychologist throughout one's career and are simply part of being a mental health professional.

The early years are often the most demanding. Common difficulties at this point include informing your client that you are a trainee, being told by clients that you are too young and inexperienced, or feeling unconfident about working with people from different backgrounds. Frequent dilemmas include: what can I as a young person possibly know about or offer this experienced older person? How can I help parents when I don't have children myself? Why did my client fail to turn up after the first session or request to speak to my supervisor? What do I do when clients depend on me, or express thoughts and wishes to harm themselves or others? When do I need to involve/consult with other professionals? Can I really take a holiday without feeling guilty?

Most clinical psychologists find ways of resolving such questions over time, adding that they gain guidance and assurance from reading and integrating scientific research findings or professional guidelines into their clinical practice. A common experience is also gradually learning to appreciate and accept the complexities of clinical decision-making. Clinical psychologists often have to intervene in complicated situations where the evidence base may be unclear, and this may therefore feel risky. Clients do not fit comfortably into categories and boxes: clients' real experiences are often much messier than we would expect from reading neat and tidy case reports in manuals and handbooks.

Key to this is learning to take account of each individual client, within their particular culture and context. For example, one newly qualified clinical psychologist, reported:

> I never expected this journey to be so personally challenging. The training has left me with more questions about myself than answers. I'm leaving the programme recognizing there is place for techniques and models in the therapy room but that place isn't paramount. The people in the room are paramount to me now, then the presenting problem and everything else. I'll just see what happens.

It might also sound surprising in a field that is all about people, but working as a clinical psychologist can sometimes feel quite lonely. At some clinical sites, you might be the only clinical psychologist working with a particular service or client group; nobody else might have experience with your supervisors or colleagues, while the many hours studying, writing, and solving statistical problems at home might make you feel isolated. Therefore, when you can get it, support from fellow clinical psychologists becomes invaluable. This might range from formally arranged peer supervision meetings to an ad hoc date in the clinical service's cafeteria when it all seems a bit too much. The newly qualified clinical psychologist also added:

> As a junior clinical psychologist I really appreciate the support I experience when meeting the other juniors on regular teaching days in the department, to blow off steam, moan about the long commute, and share experiences and anxieties about clients and supervisors.

What about more experienced clinical psychologists? Although we might be paid professionals, we are human beings too, and keeping an appropriate distance between ourselves and our clients' distressing emotional experiences between sessions can sometime be tricky. This can have both good and bad consequences. To quote Carl Jung: 'The meeting of two personalities is like the contact of two chemical substances: if there is any reaction, both are transformed.'

Being an attentive psychologist can be especially hard when clients disclose their traumatic histories (some of which may touch on you personally too). For example, it can be difficult to hear graphic histories of childhood sexual abuse when you yourself have a young child of a similar age, or maybe had some similarly traumatic experiences yourself in your own childhood. As a professional, your over-arching concern must of course be for your client, but it can sometimes be emotionally draining.

Likewise, it can be hard to hang onto feelings of hope when a client is in deep despair, possibly following a serious injury or illness, or to know exactly when to seek additional help when a client is pondering suicide.

Unfortunately, for an estimated 5 per cent of clinical psychologists who work with deeply troubled clients, excessive stress leads to so-called 'compassion fatigue', which poses a risk to both the clinical psychologist and their clients. Alternative terms are 'vicarious', 'secondary', or 'indirect' trauma. Compassion fatigue results from clinical psychologists worrying excessively about their clients, and can show itself in symptoms of stress like having trouble sleeping, nightmares, hyper-alertness and arousal, tension, and obsessive focus on a particular trauma.

We can, for example, remember a senior colleague and competent leader of a therapy group, who became numb, distant, and overwhelmed by a sense of guilt and responsibility when one of her long-term clients committed suicide and the client's family started a court case against her. This sudden suicide had required our colleague to prioritize managing the feelings of the other clients in the group, the client's family, and the staff team. At the bottom of her priority list were her own feelings of loss, anger, failure, and anxiety about losing someone whom she had been supporting for so many years. The result for her was extreme emotional exhaustion, which led her to contemplate resignation from the profession and her carefully chosen career.

A related concept is that of 'burn-out'. Burn-out is prominent across many professions including those working with psychological distress. It is associated with a lack of job fulfilment and tends to develop gradually over time, instead of having a sudden onset. Burn-out, unlike compassion fatigue, often results when individual and workplace demands don't match up. In our field, such workplace demands might include the pressure of long waiting lists, lack of resources or protected research time, having responsibility for a large number of clients, and managing colleagues' anxieties, together with the bureaucratic demands of completing daily notes, filing, assessments, and letter writing.

Someone who feels 'burned out' may start to treat clients with less compassion, feel hopeless, and be dismissive of their own and others' feelings. In a recent survey, one-third of clinical psychologists said they often feel overwhelmed with bureaucratic and unimportant tasks in their practice, adding that they experience more stress from their administrative responsibilities than from their clients. Some senior clinical psychologists also describe experiencing burn-out after many years of clinical practice, having become the emotional outlet for their junior colleagues and managers as well as for their clients.

Self-care

We can't avoid all work-related stress, but awareness of the risk factors of compassion fatigue and burn-out is an important first step. We know that there are several factors that increase the likelihood of developing symptoms of compassion fatigue, such as being female, younger, personally distressed, and less experienced, as well as having no specialized trauma training, working in an inpatient service, having heavy workloads, and working with trauma victims. Being aware of these risk factors, better self-care can have a real protective function. For example, receiving personal therapy (in past or present) probably protects against work stress, as does continued supervision and being part of a team. Feeling supported by a group of colleagues who understand your experience can be enormously important.

Also, the use of evidence-based techniques reduces burn-out and compassion fatigue and increases satisfaction, perhaps because it helps the clinical psychologist to feel more prepared and confident. Furthermore, having a broad range of roles or tasks can be protective: the chances of feeling fatigued or burned out by emotionally demanding client work is significantly reduced when you don't have all your eggs in one basket. That is, on the days when client work is stressful, it can be a relief to focus on a research project or team meeting. Or you might gain satisfaction from sharing your knowledge through teaching or supervision.

A clinical psychologist's work never stops

Despite such demands and risks, in fact most clinical psychologists don't experience compassion fatigue or burn-out in their professional career. Following training, a career in clinical psychology for most people remains fulfilling, satisfying, and continually stimulating. The majority remain in clinical practice for the rest of their working lives. There is a wide variety of ways of earning a living as a clinical psychologist, from working in large state-funded services to private practice. The focus can range from individual therapy to working with high performing leaders in industry, and from working with newborns to the very old.

Continuing in the job requires cognitive attentiveness, emotional resilience, and a sustained interest in understanding and alleviating the distress of others. Many clinical psychologists nowadays work well beyond the traditional retirement age. A large international database of thousands of clinical psychologists shows some people even working into their 90s. One very senior clinical psychologist and professor emeritus put it this way:

> I have always felt a strong desire to remain active as a clinician, even though some of my time is now taken up by managerial tasks and supervising other professionals and junior colleagues. Like many of my colleagues, I have continued to develop my professional and personal skills through my own supervision, personal therapy, and keeping updated with developments in the field through research and reading journals.

This constant sense of learning and growing throughout one's career is supported by the professional requirement for all clinical psychologists to attend continuing education events every year, such as workshops and conferences. In this way, both the profession and the bodies that regulate the professionals work together to protect the ongoing enthusiasm and commitment of clinical psychologists, and hence to protect the public who receive their services.

Chapter 6
Current agreements and debates

So far in this VSI we have examined what clinical psychologists do, where they work, whom they work with, how they think and train, who employs them, and what it feels like actually being one. In this chapter we look at what most believe to be true, and also at what is controversial. But first we must admit that as a profession, clinical psychologists are often criticized for *not* disagreeing or stating their views firmly enough.

Compared to, say judges, academics, or medical professionals, clinical psychologists don't very often express clear opinions. Most clinical psychologists seem to prefer avoiding conflict, not wanting to choose sides or confront people. Most of us won't tell you what to think, or whether what you do is right or wrong. And although it is good that clinical psychologists take this open and understanding stance, many would argue that clinical psychologists actually sit on the fence far too much.

This fence sitting has implications both for individual clients and for mental healthcare in general. For instance, on an individual level, a woman who wants concrete advice might feel really frustrated when a clinical psychologist instead encourages her to explore her own thoughts and feelings about the issue, and refuses to give clear opinions. On a more general level, the field of clinical psychology has been criticized for not promoting itself enough, and for not challenging the widespread acceptance of the psychiatric 'medicalization' of misery, that is, of seeing people who are unhappy as being 'ill'. Because clinical psychologists tend to work alongside psychiatry and use medical terminology and diagnoses, they have been accused of colluding with this illness-based model of mental health rather than promoting the view that difficult feelings are the normal consequences of dealing with the demands that life often throws at us.

Further, clinical psychologists have been criticized for being too individualistic, minimizing the importance of social or economic factors in contributing to personal distress, and for thinking of the distressed person as having the problem in coping with the world or society, rather than seeing the world or society as having the problem.

Some also argue that clinical psychology merely provides temporary individual solutions to bigger social problems such as loneliness, sexual and emotional abuse, marital breakdown, economic inequality, or the consequences of unemployment, racial prejudice, and persecution (all of which we know are strongly linked to mental health problems)—and that if we truly wanted to help people, we should really address these bigger, social issues. Helping people to understand why they feel unhappy (say through psychotherapy) might not be as helpful as challenging inequalities and discrimination in society, which might more effectively decrease the chances of people experiencing mental health difficulties in the first place.

Consequently, some argue that we should more readily speak up and campaign on wider societal issues: acting as the voice of those with psychological difficulties who may not be able or willing to speak up for themselves. If we don't take on this social responsibility, we may be failing in our role as advocates for the under-privileged, mentally distressed, or repressed in society.

Others argue however that these are broad political and social problems, which are beyond the scope of clinical psychology to resolve, since they raise questions of ideology, values, and belief, which professionals on their own cannot answer. All of us have the right as citizens to try to influence how society is organized, but some say we shouldn't let our personal or political opinions intrude on our work.

What clinical psychologists agree about

Despite these controversies, there are some core principles that all of us tend to agree on. These principles concern what clinical psychologists think causes mental health problems; how the mind works; what helps people change; and how psychological interventions can help people make these changes. Here is a short list of what clinical psychologists agree are the causes of mental health problems:

1. Most of us are strongly affected by our early childhood experiences, although we are not determined by them. Early experiences affect how we perceive other people, the world, and ourselves. We all view new relationships partly through the lenses of early important relationships.
2. A lack of consistent and caring parenting always has a negative impact, although we can recover from damaging experiences psychologically, especially if there is consistent support provided by other people in our lives.
3. Nobody can be 100 per cent happy all the time. Mental health is on a continuum and at different times in our lives, we can be anywhere on the continuum. We all struggle with our emotional experiences sometimes, but some people do experience certain emotional difficulties more intensely or more frequently than others.
4. Poverty, inequality, and trauma are bad for our mental health and affect our capacity to live psychologically healthy lives. Evidence shows that the unequal distribution of wealth and living in poverty are both linked to levels of psychological distress.
5. We all have a unique genetic make-up that interacts with our familial, social, economic, cultural environment, and life experiences

(and vice versa). Each person is therefore different, even if they seem to describe similar difficulties.

The way our mind works:

1. Nearly everyone wants to be loved and is seeking connection with other people. Most of those who feel rejected, excluded, or have low self esteem tend to blame themselves, before blaming others. This results in self-perpetuating unhappiness. Feeling connected with and supported by others are protective factors for our mental wellbeing.

2. 'Mentalization' (i.e. the capacity to understand, in ourselves and others, the wishes, feelings, beliefs, and intentions that underlie what we do) is important in protecting our mental health and, with the help of psychological interventions, can be developed by most people.

3. How we think (or make judgements) about our mental and physical health has at least as much impact on our health as objective 'facts'. To use Shakespeare's famous words: 'there is nothing either good or bad, but thinking makes it so'.

4. 'Intuition' comes first. Reasoning comes second. We often underestimate how influenced we are by our (unconscious) feelings, wrongly believing that we and other people are acting entirely rationally.

5. We tend to cope with difficulties in ways that are familiar to us—acting in ways that were helpful to us in the past, even if these ways are now ineffective or destructive.

6. Although not all emotions are comfortable or easy to feel, all emotions have a function, are meaningful, and need to be attended to.

How change occurs:

1. We all thrive when given attention, and being encouraged and praised is more effective at changing our behaviour than being punished. The best way to increase the frequency of a behaviour is to reward it.

2. 'Acting-out behaviour', whether from a child (temper tantrum) or an adult (substance misuse/self-harm), should be seen as a form of communication that needs to be understood for its meaning rather than punished.

3. Although people can't function well if they're highly distressed, experiencing some level of distress or discomfort is often necessary to achieve the motivation to change.

4. You can't make people change if they don't want to, but you can support and encourage them to make changes. Clinical psychologists work best when sitting alongside their clients in a non-judgemental, collaborative way.

How clinical psychology can help:

1. Talking about emotional experiences with another person, in and of itself, can reduce suffering in that it makes people feel more connected, and can offer relief, understanding, and insight.

2. Psychological therapy is not just about *what* clinical psychologists do. Rather, it is about who they are, who the client is, how they interact with the client, and the nature of the relationship. Most successful therapies involve an empathic therapist who listens to the client's experience, builds a safe relationship, makes meaning of the client's difficulties, creates hope, and focuses on the agreed tasks and goals for the therapy.

3. A range of psychological therapies can be effective if conducted well and are responsive to individuals. Although there is more evidence supporting some types of therapy than others, for particular difficulties, this doesn't necessarily mean other therapies are unhelpful: just that there has been less research done on them.

What clinical psychologists disagree about

Most professions that include lots of passionate individuals come with a multitude of opinions, debates, and discussions. The field of clinical psychology is no different, even if the arguments are sometimes muted. Here we have chosen to focus on three such controversies, although there are undoubtedly also others.

- How reflective should clinical psychologists be; should we have to undergo our own personal therapy?
- We say we are scientist-practitioners (see Chapters 1 and 3), but can clinical psychologists really claim to be scientists?
- In practice, what should clinical psychologists focus their efforts on?

Being reflective

Historically, from the early, Freudian days, seeking to self-reflect and to undergo personal therapy was integral to a career as a mental health professional. Subsequently, however, some clinical psychologists have argued that we should not engage in personal therapy because this might distract us from the task of becoming detached scientists, diverting us into self-examination, self-indulgence, and subjectivity. Nowadays, however, about half of Western clinical psychologists do see personal therapy as essential, and 75 per cent of clinical psychologists have received some form of personal therapy (although this differs between theoretical models: psychoanalytic clinicians have the highest rates and behaviour therapists the lowest).

There are several arguments in favour of clinical psychologists having personal therapy, usually as part of their training. First, clients are not the only people who bring their past into the consulting room. When we as clinical psychologists experience emotional reactions to clients (as we inevitably do), we need to know if this reveals something specific about this particular client or whether it has more to do with our own personal history. The more we understand ourselves and what triggers us, the better we can resist re-enacting our own personal patterns with our clients. If we truly want to understand our clients' subjective experiences, we need to understand ourselves too: which feeling belongs to whom? Therapy should help with this.

Second, we as clinical psychologists are human beings too, and personal therapy might help us overcome our own internal struggles (e.g. insecurities and self-image issues) and to address our external problems (e.g. with our families and work), thus improving our own lives and making us more compassionate, balanced, and open-minded. In this sense, personal therapy is a part of self-care, making sure we are as psychologically healthy as we can be.

Third, in order for clinical psychologists to create hope, they need to believe in the potential benefit of psychological work. If we experience personal therapy as helpful ourselves, this might convince us of its validity, demonstrating its transformational power in our own lives. Arguably, if clinical psychologists don't believe that they themselves could benefit from the therapeutic tools of their profession, they have no business practising them on others!

Last, it could be helpful for clinical psychologists to experience being a client first-hand. As one of our colleagues said: 'Personal therapy made me realize how frightening it can be to open up to a therapist. My respect for my clients has increased dramatically as a result.' Psychodynamic therapist Nancy McWilliams also eloquently commented:

> I approached treatment cerebrally, as the obvious thing to do for professional reasons…[Yet], I found myself trembling with a child's anxiety about safety…. I felt exposed, out of control, vulnerable to being criticized and shamed. And I wasn't even coming for a 'disorder'…I was completely out of touch with any personal need for therapy…

Arguments against clinical psychologists having personal therapy include the lack of firm evidence that this has a direct, positive effect on treatment outcomes for their clients, and the difficulty in making something so personal a compulsory part of training. Not all clinical psychologists decide to work as therapists: some may work mostly in assessment, or in management or legal services, or as teachers or researchers, so it may be less relevant for them. Of course it is also expensive, and arguably wasteful, to spend scarce resources on people who don't really feel they have any serious mental health problems themselves. There are also some ethical concerns about possibly exposing people to the discomfort and challenge that might emerge during therapy. Instead, 'virtual' or vicarious experiences of the client role (e.g. in structured role-play or through extensive viewing of live or video-taped sessions) could be sufficient for some trainees to gain some of the benefits of personal therapy. There are no definite answers to these questions, so the debate continues.

Claiming to be scientists

There are currently two closely related and influential scientific developments in the mental health field (including clinical psychology): evidence-based practice (EBP), originating in the UK; and empirically supported treatments (EST), originating in the USA. These two developments aspire to integrate the best available scientific evidence concerning what helps people, with clinical experience and with individual client preferences or values. Central to both developments is the scientific method as a way of advancing knowledge.

Consequently, governmental organizations and insurance companies (who pay for health services) are increasingly requiring clinical psychologists and other mental health researchers to demonstrate that psychological treatments are based on empirical, scientific evidence, and to prove that they work. This has in turn led to attempts by governments and insurance companies to mandate the types of treatment that must be provided by practicing clinical psychologists.

These movements have been mostly welcomed by clinical psychologists in the field, all of whom have originally been trained according to the research traditions of academic, scientific psychology. Furthermore, conducting research is now seen as a key role for clinical psychologists, as demonstrated by professional guidelines and job descriptions. For example, the 2013 NHS careers website stated that 'due to their high level of research skills, clinical psychologists undertake the role of scientist-practitioner, as an innovator and applied researcher, adding to the evidence base of practice in a variety of health care settings'.

Most clinical psychologists see psychology as a science, and adhere to research as 'a core state of mind'. This has been good for both clinical psychology and its clients. By using scientific methods and drawing on peer-reviewed robust evidence, clinical psychologists have gained a considerable amount of knowledge about many mental health conditions, and how they develop or change. This has enabled them to introduce effective treatments and interventions for a wide range of people, based on empirical research.

This emphasis on research does not however translate whole-heartedly into everyday reality. Most trainees probably choose the profession because of their keen interest in people, not because they primarily wanted to 'do' research. Many of them actually experience anxiety and ambivalence about the requirements of conducting scientific research themselves, possibly seeing their required dissertation research as a rather necessary evil. The title of a popular student website 'www.statisticshell.com' gives a flavour of how research was (and maybe still is) perceived within some parts of the profession. And even post-qualification, the majority of clinical psychologists, although well trained and able to do so, do not actually become active researchers themselves. Most never publish a single study beyond their doctoral dissertation, that is, if they publish their dissertation projects at all, often citing the challenging process of doing so (see Figure 5).

5. Publishing in a peer-reviewed journal is a process with many hurdles.

Besides not conducting or publishing research themselves, there are also significant disagreements within the profession about the strength of evidence for specific psychological models, and some controversy about accepting the pressure of providing only EBP- or EST-based interventions. Some practitioners have been reluctant to change how they work despite new evidence from academic researchers suggesting different ways of doing things (especially when the new ways are included in manuals, which tell the clinical psychologist, step-by-step, what they should be doing with specific client groups).

So we must ask: why do some clinical psychologists who call themselves scientists, and say they value science, not apparently behave like scientists? There are a number of possible answers. Most importantly, the problem is that most academic researchers in clinical psychology, like those in other scientific fields, strive to extract universal or quasi-universal 'rules' that will apply in all circumstances. Such 'rules' tend to be included in manuals, beloved by funding agencies, which specify what needs to be done by practitioners.

Yet the everyday task of clinical psychologists concerns individuals who differ from one another in terms of values, beliefs, problems, personal preferences, family circumstances, relationship styles, and cultures. Practitioners deal with the unique case, and are confronted with the exceedingly difficult task of applying group-based research findings to the individual in front of them. Clients frequently don't seem to fit neatly into the boxes described in the textbooks. Practitioners don't therefore always find scientific research results (or manuals) to be that applicable or helpful. Instead many say they prefer to learn from qualitative studies or case reports.

There are also some practical reasons for practitioners not conducting much research themselves, including the complexity involved in conducting good studies, and the need to follow bureaucratic ethics or governance processes. For those employed in public services, protected research time is usually a luxury, since the requirements of doing clinical work soon swamp psychologists' ability to reserve time for scientific research. And for those who are self-employed, conducting research may lead to reduced income, since doing research may restrict time available for appointments. Being a reflective scientist-practitioner actually turns out to be a considerable practical challenge.

In parallel there are arguments about whether clinical psychology is more art than science anyway—how research should be conducted, and what designs and analyses are best. See for example Box 21 for the pros and cons of conducting randomized controlled trials, and Box 22 for opinions about qualitative analyses.

Perhaps the best way to resolve these questions is for us to accept that, in reality, all psychological research is flawed. Different research methods have different pros and cons, and no matter what, all research only reveals an approximation of the truth.

Box 21 What is the value of randomized controlled trials?

Conducting research into the effect of psychological therapies with randomized controlled trials (RCTs) has many advantages. RCTs are studies that attempt to keep as many variables as possible the same (controlled) between two groups, except for one variable: the type of therapy being studied. The people being studied are allocated between the two groups randomly, so any difference in the results obtained should not have been caused by pre-existing differences between participants. The treatment is also manualized. This helps researchers to conclude which therapy is more effective.

Despite the advantages of this design, however, RCTs also have shortcomings. Critics claim that these trials often only include easy and simple cases that differ from more complex cases that are normally seen in routine practice. RCTs also implicitly assume that clients with similar formulations or diagnoses are similar and that they will respond the same way to the same treatment. In reality, it is rare that there is only one difference (the type of therapy) between two groups. We know for example that different psychologists don't work exactly the same as one another even if they apply the same treatment, and also that the same psychologist does not behave identically with each and every client in each session.

We will never know with 100 per cent certainty that a particular therapy, procedure, or psychologist will be beneficial for this particular new client. Therefore we must do our best to combine research findings, pull information together, and creatively complete different parts of the puzzle about what helps clients most effectively. In that sense, qualitative research has as much potential to inform clinical psychology as quantitative research programmes, such as larger scale RCTs.

Box 22 What is the use of qualitative analyses?

Roughly speaking, quantitative studies use numbers and statistics while qualitative studies make an argument from case descriptions or coherent narratives. When Freud established his theories of the human psyche in the late 19th century, he wrote not only theoretical papers, but also a number of qualitative case studies, descriptions of clients, their conversations, and notes about his own experience, as the therapist, to illustrate his points. At the time, these were hugely influential. But psychology as a discipline has since then largely dismissed this method of investigation, seeing it as biased and unreliable.

Instead, quantitative work using statistics and numerical analysis of data have become dominant in clinical psychology, as in most social sciences. Nowadays qualitative research is often seen as non-scientific, weaker, and less publishable, and is slightly frowned upon by 'real' (quantitative) researchers. Critics of qualitative research say it risks being biased, unreliable, and only applicable to small numbers of people. Official guidelines consequently prioritize findings from quantitative studies, such as large scale RCTs.

The advantage of qualitative research, however, is that it can explore topics in depth, and can provide a closer, more nuanced account of the subjective experience of clients. Some psychologists see it as more practical and closer to real interactions than sets of figures reported in quantitative papers. Consequently, some clinicians find qualitative research papers more illuminating than quantitative papers, and easier to translate into their clinical work with clients. Some psychologists also think it provides a better way of looking at complex questions like personal meaning and experience, relationships and cultural diversity, and can help build understanding of rare cases and conditions.

Focusing our clinical efforts

Besides these controversies on being reflective and scientific, our clinical practice raises another important area of debate: when working with clients, should we focus on providing specific techniques, or on more general supportive factors like hope, kindness, and listening skills? The problem is that we know that clinical psychological interventions can be effective, but we don't yet know exactly why.

A good example is that the positive therapeutic relationship has been demonstrated in numerous research studies to be linked to good treatment outcome. But does the positive relationship lead to the good outcome, or vice versa? Is it technique, or is it courteous attention from a professional person with good listening skills? Are sessions actually pretty similar across different types of therapy, even though what happens in these sessions might have different labels? Or is the process different, but actually this doesn't matter because the outcome is the same anyway?

There are several different views on this question. Cognitive therapists, for example, argue that it is the client making cognitive changes in how they think that leads to improvements, and that this then enhances the relationship between client and therapist. Others, like some psychodynamically oriented therapists, believe it is the positive therapeutic relationship that then allows the client to make the cognitive changes. Separating out the different components in real time, given all the other factors going on, makes this very hard to prove one way or another. In fact, the answer is probably quite complex.

Although a lot still needs to be discovered, some findings have become clearer over time. For example, we know that neither specific therapy techniques nor general factors are wholly responsible for the benefits of psychological interventions. Instead, a large body of evidence shows that psychological therapies work through a combination of general helpful factors (like having hope, a positive expectation of change, being listened to, coming to a new understanding about things, opening up channels of communication), *and* some specific interventions derived from psychological theories (like Socratic questioning, behavioural experiments, changing structures within the family, or gaining insight into repeated relationship patterns; see Chapter 3).

We also know that all psychologists and their clients need to establish positive working relationships in order for their work together to be effective. This involves agreeing about tasks and goals, and having an appropriate emotional bond. It isn't necessary to adhere slavishly to specific treatment protocols, but an intervention must contain more than common factors alone. Clients expect and need coherent explanations for their distress, and they benefit most when this explanation and rationale is consistent with their own worldview.

All theoretical orientations can offer words, strategies, and images that may help people make changes. But sensing which will work, when, and for whom (and knowing how to implement this) is the essential art of clinical psychology. In parallel, using techniques, evidence, and theory to inform the practicing psychologist's intuition is what comprises the science. The debate around the importance of specific techniques is also reflected in the differences in professional training and internships across different countries (see Box 23).

This chapter has devoted a bit more space to disagreements than agreements within clinical psychology. But we don't see this as a negative thing. Conflicting viewpoints usually help disciplines to develop and build improvements in both their theories and future practice. Indeed the next (and final) chapter of this VSI concerns the future, and also reviews some recent developments that seem likely to take clinical psychology further in its quest to balance science with concern for individual health and wellbeing.

Box 23 Training in specific techniques or general skills?

Some argue psychologists must thoroughly learn one therapeutic
model and its techniques before trying to integrate it with other
models, methods, and techniques. This might mean learning
to use a particular therapy manual and practicing techniques
extensively with similar clients, untill the psychologist grows
confident and competent. In the USA for example, you can
choose to become really knowledgeable about one particular
therapy model or client group. However, the risk of (only)
knowing one model/approach is that you may be tempted
to apply it to every client you see, even if this isn't optimal for
a particular client or problem.

Others argue therefore that rather than focusing on one
particular model or client type, you should gain a wide range of
clinical experiences and build your transferable general
therapeutic skills. In the UK, for example, trainees are allocated
placements in diverse services with a range of clients. This results
in generalizable skills, more knowledge of the different services,
problems, clients, and ways of working, but might also make
trainees feel 'a jack of all trades and a master of none'.

Chapter 7
Extending the reach of clinical psychology

By now, you will have a fair idea of what clinical psychologists can do and how they currently contribute to healthcare. But roles are developing, and the field of clinical psychology is expanding across national boundaries. Social priorities are evolving and the profession is changing in response. Clinical psychologists' skills are also developing, linked to advances in medicine, communication, technology, and science. This final chapter examines the wider scope and possible future directions of the profession.

The profession's international contribution

The field of clinical psychology is not restricted by national boundaries: clinical psychologists work mostly in Western countries like Europe, the USA, and Australia, but also in growing numbers in Asia, Africa, and the Middle East. There are numerous variations in how clinical psychologists work internationally that naturally reflect different national cultures and traditions. Research findings are shared at international conferences and published in academic journals that are accessible online throughout the globe, although interpreted and applied according to local circumstances and needs.

Clinical psychologists have made a significant difference to people in many different countries and cultures. For example clinical psychologists in Japan have worked closely with children and their families who survived the major earthquake in 2011, encouraging survivors to re-build their lives. Clinical psychologists in war-torn Rwanda have provided structures for reconciliation efforts, and also therapies for children and families who have been severely affected by violence. In Congo, clinical psychologists have focused on empowering and training local colleagues to work in conflict situations, while British clinical psychologists have helped to set up training courses in Uganda, Trinidad, Tobago, and Bangladesh.

Some clinical psychologists work across the world in international organizations like UNICEF, the Red Cross, and the World Health Organization. Clinical psychologists also contribute to military programmes in Libya, Iraq, Afghanistan, and Yemen for soldiers who are serving overseas, and afterwards as veterans in their home countries. Other international examples include programmes to decrease domestic violence in Sierra Leona, and to provide services in a number of West African countries supporting those living with HIV/AIDS.

A further example of an influential international programme implemented by clinical psychologists is the needle-exchange programme for drug users. While the initial programme originated in the Netherlands in the 1980s following an outbreak of hepatitis B, the AIDS pandemic then motivated a rapid adoption of these initiatives around the world. The programme promotes harm reduction: acknowledging that drug abuse is a reality in society, while aiming to minimize the damage associated with drug use and to reduce the risk factors for diseases such as HIV/AIDS and hepatitis B. Needle exchange programmes allow injecting drug users to have access to clean needles and associated injection equipment such as alcohol swabs and sterilized water, at little or no cost. Many of these programmes also offer free health education and counselling.

Despite our increasingly global society, and the shared use of the title 'clinical psychologist', it is perhaps unsurprising that different countries still have very different patterns of education and training. A globally agreed standard of qualification for clinical psychology training is a long way off. For clinical psychologists, practising clinically abroad is often limited through local licensing requirements, exams, and legal restrictions. These are linked to national differences in health systems, educational systems, culture, governmental focus, and language barriers, as well as to how clinical psychologists are paid (i.e. whether they work for public services, for large or small private organizations, or primarily for individual clients and families).

There are also large variations internationally in what clinical psychologists see as their central focus and purpose. This ranges from self-development, self-care, and prevention on one end of the spectrum, to diagnosis, treatment, and cure of severe mental disorders or illness at the other end. For example, as already noted, clinical psychologists in Argentina have a longstanding tradition of providing psychological treatment to people who wish to understand themselves better or improve their quality of life—looking for positive changes that will promote a sense of personal growth and accomplishment. Although some will initially seek the help for difficulties that might meet formal diagnostic criteria for a 'disorder' or illness (e.g. an 'anxiety disorder' or 'adjustment disorder' as classified in the psychiatric diagnostic manuals DSM-V or ICD-10), they usually continue therapy even after achieving full remission of their symptoms, since their view of psychotherapy is not restricted to the notion of 'recovery'.

By contrast, in countries such as the UK, USA, or Canada, most clients will present with difficulties that could probably be labelled as 'illness' or 'disorder', and therapeutic contact would normally cease once this has been resolved. Certainly, in many countries, clients seeking personal growth would not usually be eligible for funded services, since their degree of clinical suffering would not meet full diagnostic criteria.

Changing roles

Alongside international developments, the profession of clinical psychology is also changing its role and remit within most national systems. In many countries there are widespread and influential changes in how much funding is available for mental healthcare, and a growing need to provide equitable access to services while also containing costs. So while more people are being encouraged to seek psychological support (which might benefit them), in most places there are also real shortages in numbers of doctoral-level trained clinical psychologists, and a dramatic reduction in insurance or public funds available for reimbursement of mental health services.

This set of circumstances has led to increasing numbers of other services offering alternative (cheaper) forms of psychologically informed mental healthcare. These vary from therapies provided by trained professionals, such as nurses or counsellors working under the supervision of clinical psychologists, to various groups of untrained or alternative therapists who undoubtedly don't have the range of competencies that clinical psychologists have. And although we don't feel overly pessimistic, there is definitely a trend (within healthcare more generally) for work to be shifted to people with fewer formal qualifications. For example, many tasks previously done by medical doctors are now being done by nurse practitioners. Many services previously provided by nurses are now being offered by nursing assistants.

It seems probable therefore that the balance of work now being done by clinical psychologists will change in the future. Although psychotherapy isn't likely to disappear from the job description, our pre-eminence in that arena has probably peaked and will not return. We suspect that Master's-level practitioners under a variety of labels (e.g. licensed professional counsellors, mental health counsellors, marriage and family therapists), and volunteers with limited training, may well become the dominant providers of psychotherapy in the future. In many publically funded models of care, the skills of clinical psychologists will probably be reserved for complex problems that don't respond to simpler interventions.

These changes are positive in many ways, if they make psychological treatment more routinely accessible and cost-effective, and assuming that there are enough clinical psychologists available to work with more complex cases. But if Master's-level providers (or indeed anyone else in the healthcare sector) are going to take the lead in the delivery of psychotherapy for the majority of cases, then what will tomorrow's clinical psychologists do?

As we hope we have shown earlier in this VSI, this should not be a problem. Clinical psychologists are not just psychotherapists since they also work as supervisors, consultants, trainers, evaluators, and leaders of clinical or research teams or institutions. There are many possible ways of working to improve people's psychological wellbeing, and the rest of this chapter will outline a number of promising future directions.

Organizational work and leadership

Increasing numbers of clinical psychologists in healthcare organizations now work not only with clients but also with the staff, either to increase the wellbeing of colleagues or to build better ways for staff to work together. Some clinical psychologists now provide sessions for their colleagues designed to help distressed staff to continue to provide care despite the emotional load. Others work with teams, designed to build more effective working environments (see the examples in Box 24).

Yet other clinical psychologists work as team leaders or service managers, seeing their role as enhancing the work of others. Some

Box 24 Supporting colleagues and supporting teams

David's job was to provide help for colleagues who worked in a unit for brain-injured patients who were sometimes violent and abusive towards other patients or the staff who cared for them. While most staff had developed ways of coping with this challenge, Paula, a new trainee nurse, was particularly upset by an episode where a young man had hit an elderly resident, following which Paula had requested an immediate transfer from the unit, despite the negative impact this might have had on her training. David provided some time for Paula who revealed that the older man was strongly reminiscent of her grandfather who had recently passed away, and had (Paula believed) been rather unjustly treated by the rest of the family. With David's help, Paula decided to continue to work at the brain injury unit, while David persuaded the management to provide more regular supervision meetings for the whole staff team.

Sara had just started work in a small team of social and healthcare staff, whose role was to provide care for vulnerable children where there had been some suspicion of abuse. The team operated under high levels of stress and was sometimes under attack from the local media over its handling of tricky cases. Sickness levels were high in the team and relationships between colleagues were poor. Feeling unsure of the team, staff stopped attending meetings, cliques formed, and communication deteriorated. Unsurprisingly, services for the children then suffered. So Sara set up a series of team meetings to focus on how the team itself worked, which revealed high levels of confusion about the team's aims, priorities, and structure. Drawing on research on how to set up effective teams, Sara guided the staff team to improve its ways of working by agreeing to a set of aims, objectives, structures, and operating rules, and hence indirectly improving the care provided for the children and their families.

may primarily provide clinical leadership, helping their colleagues to reflect on and improve their clinical interventions with clients, while others may provide organizational leadership, working on strategy, organizational development, and resource allocation.

Taking on more responsibilities: prescribing medication

Within most societies, and despite what we know about the value of psychological therapies, prescribed medication is still the most widespread treatment used worldwide for psychological distress. Many clients who consult clinical psychologists also make use of medication to help them to reduce their level of psychological distress. Medication undoubtedly helps many clients with mental health difficulties, by reducing the intensity of crises and taking the edge off difficult feelings, enabling people to continue to function in daily life. Although clients often experience side effects from medication (including numbing of feelings, which can make therapy more difficult), in some circumstances medication can help clients make better use of psychological therapy. For these reasons, many psychologists believe that combining medical and psychological treatments could be a valid option for many clients.

While this combination can often be straightforward, coordination of service providers is sometimes poor. It may require clients to attend multiple appointments, incurring additional expenditure and taking up extra time. The overloaded work schedules of many psychiatrists means they may have to make decisions following short interactions with clients, often narrowly focused on assessment of symptoms. Involving several professionals can also be confusing in that clients might receive contradictory advice.

All of these points have led to the call for clinical psychologists to have 'prescribing privileges' and in the USA, a public health initiative (the Prescriptive Authority for Psychologists (RxP) movement) gives prescriptive authority to specifically trained psychologists. In line with this, laws have been implemented in some US states (e.g. New Mexico in 2002; Louisiana in 2004; Illinois in 2014) to enable clinical psychologists who have attended several years of additional training and supervision to prescribe psychotropic medications to treat mental and emotional disorders. In these states, clinical psychologists have taken on some of the responsibilities of psychiatrists.

There are pros and cons to this development. Some clinical psychologists believe that such privileges will harm the practice of clinical psychology and possibly clients, while others consider that their practice options will be helpfully widened given the option of prescribing medication. The argument is complex. On the one hand, psychiatrists are undoubtedly best equipped to prescribe medication, having had intensive training in the working of the brain and body, and being familiar with potential benefits and side-effects of a variety of psychiatric medications. Psychologists might be much less aware of these aspects. Also, if clinical psychologists were able to prescribe, this might radically alter the nature of the clinical psychologist–client relationship or give the implicit message to clients that their feelings are wrong or bad, or need to be removed rather than understood.

On the other hand, the clinical psychologist might be the professional who knows the client and their circumstances best, and can judge most sensitively when medication might help and when it should be stopped. Particularly in less urbanized and therefore under-resourced areas, where clients have little or no access to psychiatrists, a clinical psychologist might be the only person who has regular contact with the client. In some places, taking on the prescribing privileges of physicians and psychiatrists could be an important way of helping people who have no other access to mental health treatment. Only time will tell whether or not this will be a sustained and successful development within clinical psychology.

Expansion of clinical health psychology

A growing area within the profession is clinical health psychology
(i.e. the application of clinical psychology principles and practices
within physical healthcare settings). Opportunities in this field
seem almost unlimited when one considers the percentage of
the gross national product in most developed countries that is
spent annually on healthcare. In fact, in the last decade, clinical
psychologists have increasingly been employed in general
hospitals and/or clinics providing healthcare for physical
problems. Other employment growth areas have been in medical
schools and academic healthcare centres, where people have
increasingly recognized the importance of psychological factors
in all aspects of physical and mental health.

The translation of cognitive science into psychological interventions
is likely to open up a variety of new treatments for people with
health-related conditions, such as computerized rehabilitation
programmes for the disabled or brain-injured. Advances in
surgical and medical procedures, together with a greater
appreciation of psychology, mean that clinical psychologists will
likely play a greater role in surgical work, for instance in assessing
and treating transplant patients. Questions include: is this patient
psychologically suitable for this operation? Can they manage
the emotional load of accepting a donor organ? Will they be able
to adhere to treatment requirements?

Other recent opportunities for clinical health psychologists include
participating in surgical teams when a patient can't tolerate
anaesthesia, helping patients and families make decisions about
genetic testing, and developing memory aids for stroke patients. The
growth of services for parents and babies in the perinatal period
(e.g. addressing problems with fertility, termination, abortion,
pregnancy, and postpartum depression) is also remarkable and is
likely to expand (see the clinical example in Box 25).

Box 25 Clinical psychologists in perinatal services

Maria and Edwin are parents who had sadly lost their 4-month-old son Joseph to sudden infant death syndrome (SIDS). At first Maria was unable to function. She cried inconsolably, hardly interacting with anyone, including her 2-year-old twins, Kim and Jennifer. Edwin, feeling the social pressures on a man to be strong, pushed his own grief aside, focused on providing for his family, and eventually coaxed his wife out of bed and back into family life.

With support from a clinical psychologist who visited her at home, Maria slowly began to consider life without Joseph. She spoke about the importance of giving birth to a boy in her family, and the sense of punishment she experienced from her religion. Although Joseph had died, she held onto his memory and wanted him to remain a part of her family. Over several months, the clinical psychologist talked with Maria alone, as well as together with Edwin and the twins. While looking at family photos one year after their loss, Maria and Edwin explained to the twins, in a way that 3-year-olds would understand, why their brother had died. On the anniversary of the death, they took Kim and Jennifer to visit the cemetery and encouraged them to ask questions about Joseph.

Maria become more willing to seek out information and support to help herself and her family cope with the loss. Drawing on the resources available to bereaved parents, they joined a support group for SIDS families and felt less alone in their experience of grief. Maria still struggles some days, and sometimes feels anxious about the unpredictability of life. However, she now seeks out people when she needs help, and focuses on strengthening her relationship with those who are most important to her.

Prevention and public health

Not all clinical psychologists work in offices or hospitals with their own individual clients. Recent innovations led by clinical psychologists have included establishing programmes that affect entire communities such as schemes designed to reduce bullying in schools or incidents of spousal abuse; establishing more effective protocols for treating addictions; developing better implementation strategies for existing treatment programmes, and setting up internet therapy services. As shown in Chapter 6, some argue that clinical psychologists could benefit clients as much by making such long-term efforts to improve treatments and social institutions (e.g. schools and social policy) as by providing individual psychotherapy. Given clinical psychologists' training and existing roles in mental health services, the profession is potentially in a good position to have significant impact on the community, and to work on prevention via structural changes in welfare provision and community wellbeing.

Clinical psychology in the community is and will continue to be very heavily influenced by the politics of the day and the economics of mental distress. Although the social context is, in some senses, outside the remit of the individual professional, the discipline as a whole acknowledges the clear link between social/economic circumstances and mental distress. Questions remain regarding the precise nature of distress caused by austerity, job losses, or poor housing. However, recently, politicians and economists have been much more willing to talk about wellbeing as a goal of policy. Interventions focusing on self-care, seeking support, and building resilience could help the individual to weather an often-hostile social environment. Doubtless this will be an important avenue in the future of the discipline.

Expansion of research focus

All healthcare services need to know if what they are providing is effective and how best to improve care for their clients. This is quite right: after all, if you or I were entering treatment of any kind—especially if it were for the first time—we would probably like to know that it was reasonably likely to be successful, and that someone had done some research on its chances of succeeding with people like us. Clinical psychology has over the decades played a pivotal role in evaluating the effectiveness and efficiency of psychological treatments through conducting good quality outcome research studies. These have improved services, saved money, and helped in the development of treatment protocols, thus ensuring that more people get access to therapies that have been proven to work.

It is highly likely that this research role will grow in importance in future decades since those who fund services (e.g. managed care in the USA and the NHS in the UK; see Chapter 6) increasingly demand evidence that those services are cost-effective. Clinical psychologists will also likely make increasing use of a number of more sophisticated research methodologies, for example using frame-by-frame filming technology that enables researchers to examine what happens when a brain-injured patient tries to communicate, or using brain scans to measure the impact of different types of therapeutic intervention.

Undoubtedly psychological research will also increasingly involve cross-fertilization of ideas and findings from other related fields. In particular, progress is likely to be made at the interface between psychotherapy research and neuroscience, as knowledge about brain functioning consolidates and develops. Genetics will also play an increasingly central role. In addition, detailed research on the basic psychological processes that underlie mental health problems, and on how people communicate and build relationships, will open up new possibilities by making use of powerful computer-assisted methodologies.

We believe that clinical research will become increasingly specialist, drawing on existing work on client–treatment matching

that takes account of both client and psychologist characteristics
that may be associated with positive therapy outcome. We
anticipate that future research will enable us to learn more about
the individual variables involved in more or less successful
interventions for different kinds of clients.

Use of technology

Technology is seeping into the clinical psychology world,
just like everywhere else. Technological developments are
enabling new forms and formats for assessment and intervention,
including online recruitment for research, online testing,
therapy, and supervision. One example of a recent innovation is
the development of storytelling video games that provide a
motivational and immersive experience for children with autism
who have trouble communicating. Such games can develop
the children's social skills and subsequently improve their
daily interactions.

Another example is the introduction of virtual reality scenarios
for treating people with social phobia. These scenarios can
be designed specifically to expose people to particular social
situations that trigger their anxiety (i.e. giving a talk or
going shopping). People can engage in a free speech dialogue with
avatars while being monitored by a clinical psychologist, who can
then adapt the avatar's response to the client by controlling the
avatar's gaze or dialogue style as well as what happens to the
avatar during the interaction or experience.

Virtual reality technology can also provide access to situations that
are otherwise difficult (or costly) to access, such as flying. Instead
of boarding a real plane in order to confront a fear of flying, a
person can simply put on a headset and a pair of headphones that
simulate the experience. Numbers of people treated can thereby
be increased while costs will fall.

Probably the most widespread application of technology in clinical psychology concerns how therapy is provided. While in Freudian times, having analysis a few times a week on the couch in the analyst's consulting rooms might have been standard, nowadays people can access therapy via Skype, through mental health apps, or online individualized psychological programmes. Some clinical psychologists see clients face-to-face most of the time but might use Skype or phone sessions in an emergency (see Box 26), while others don't even have a physical office and see all their clients online. As one of our colleagues explained:

> I engineered my practice this way to make it easier for people with
> physical disabilities to see me. With Skype, my clients can stay in
> the comfort of their own homes and don't have to worry about
> travelling, or any problems in physically getting to my office.

Other technological developments include a variety of mental health applications on mobile devices: apps like Joyable, Sleepio, Happify, SuperBetter, PTSD coach, CodeBlue, TalkSpace, and PersonalZen. Some clinical psychologists welcome these new developments with open arms, given their low cost, accessibility, opportunity to reduce stigma, and potential to provide more services to more people. Such apps can be especially helpful, for

Box 26 Maya's therapy over Skype

Maya came to the approach through geographical necessity. When Simon, her long-term psychologist, moved to a new city, Maya was apprehensive about transferring to another psychologist in her small town, as he or she would almost certainly know her prominent ex-boyfriend. So Simon offered Maya Skype sessions from his new home several hundred miles away. Maya was willing to give it a try.

example, for teenagers and young adults who are suffering from serious mental health conditions, and who may be familiar with the use of technology as a means of communication, but who are unwilling or unable to attend face-to-face sessions. Such apps can also provide support between sessions and probably work best when used in conjunction with face-to-face contact (and medication if appropriate). Others are more sceptical about this 'pseudo therapy' (see Figure 6) and are troubled by what they call a misguided, quick-fix approach to mental health, where people are promised speedy relief sometimes based on limited evidence.

Besides questions of effectiveness, online services raise questions about the therapeutic relationship, ethics, confidentiality, and

6. Using technology to communicate.

licensing. No matter what your opinion, the provision of online therapy and tele-therapy is likely to expand, as technology improves.

Use of social media

Clinical psychologists may be well trained in reviewing and conducting research, but they don't get much training on how to communicate their findings to other professionals, clients, family members, or the general public. Moreover, most clinical psychologists are less comfortable working with the media or writing blogs than listening and responding to individuals. But with social media emerging as one of the best ways to share psychological research and promote clinical services to the public, some clinical psychologists are starting to become less reticent. The main requirement for those who want to be effective online is to learn to communicate well: to write clearly, in a jargon-free, concise way—whether it's a tweet, a status update, a YouTube video, or whatever ingenious new technology is coming next.

For example, a clinical psychologist in the USA, Dr Kolmes, has made imaginative use of her professional Twitter account. First, she had a blog on social media ethics, and began sharing her posts and other mental health news. Then she released a social media policy that she had developed originally to guide her own online therapy practice, which was also disseminated on Twitter. This quickly gained the attention of mental health professionals worldwide, who were seeking guidance on the topic. Within just a couple of years, Kolmes became a sought-after expert and speaker on social media ethics and her Twitter following grew to 86,500 at @drkkolmes. She published an article in *The New York Times* about the challenges of consumer review sites for psychotherapists and is a frequent news source for the media.

The use of social media enables clinical psychologists to reach a population of potential clients who were traditionally harder to reach: not only younger people but also men and less 'psychologically minded' people. Social media may help us to chip away at the stigma of mental health and its treatments, and alert people to the potential benefits of seeking psychological help. One of our colleagues in the USA aims to demystify psychotherapy on her blog with the catchy name: 'analysisissexy', and by posting on popular websites such as 'psychedinsanfrancisco'.

Another example of a popular psychology researcher who has been making maximum use of the internet is Brené Brown. She has been researching experiences like vulnerability, shame, courage, and authenticity, and has been communicating her findings in a very genuine and accessible way via several Tedtalks, available on YouTube. Her TEDxHouston Talk on vulnerability has been viewed over six million times. Interestingly, the morning after Brene gave this talk she apparently locked herself in her house for three days with a 'vulnerability hangover', which she then described in a later talk on shame. There is a lesson here: such things can happen to any of us!

Continuous evolution

Clinical psychology has come a long way in a short time. We hope that this little book has enabled you to understand how it developed, to assess its current contribution to individuals and the wider society, and to consider its future potential. One of the traditional strengths of clinical psychologists is their use of critical thinking, their application of flexible problem-solving techniques and a range of methodological research skills. Evidence for this flexibility comes from the myriad places in which clinical psychologists are found. They are employed in virtually any industry one can name (health, entertainment, education, space exploration, police work, communications) and they hold a plethora of positions that seventy years ago no-one would have thought possible.

Clinical psychology has an inherently evolving nature because it continually uses research and the scientific method to develop a better understanding of the assessment and treatment of psychological phenomena and problems. This ongoing evolving nature is reflected in its relationship with the high-tech standards of modern medicine and neuroscience, which continue to unearth new discoveries about the human brain and its connection to thought and behaviour. The future of clinical psychology will undoubtedly include more refined answers about the connection between mind and body, and will most likely continue to integrate methods and knowledge from disciplines such as medicine, genetics, sociology, and epidemiology.

Some clinical psychologists might feel daunted by the possibility of other professionals taking on aspects of their original role, and by their continuous need to adapt to research findings and opportunities, such as those presented by the social media and new technologies. But if one constructs a list of the principal problems facing the world today, there is one inescapable conclusion: a large proportion of people's struggles have a psychological component.

The leading killers at the beginning of the 20th century (viral and bacterial illnesses such as pneumonia, tuberculosis, and influenza) have been replaced in many parts of the world today by cancer, heart disease, depression, and stroke. These are all conditions heavily influenced by behavioural or psychosocial factors, such as smoking, poor eating habits, lack of exercise, and stress. Similarly, some of the critically important societal problems that face the world today are strongly influenced by psychology: inequality, domestic or interpersonal conflict, poor parenting, divorce, addiction, educational dysfunction, crime, racism, obesity, employee stress and dissatisfaction, loneliness, abuse, pollution, and the overuse of environmental resources.

The science and practice of psychology, especially clinical psychology, could play a key part in the development and application of solutions to some of these problems. Clinical psychology possesses an unique combination of features which makes it perfectly placed to contribute to the development of solutions to some of the urgent and widespread challenges currently facing society, besides attending to people's intimate and highly individual personal experiences. The clinical psychologist who is trained as a reflective scientist-practitioner should have no difficulty finding both worthwhile and necessary things to do in the future. We hope that our changing world will also gain from clinical psychologists' continuing attention, thinking, commitment, and action.

References and further reading

Barker, C., Pistrang, N., & Elliott, R., *Research Methods in Clinical Psychology: An Introduction for Students and Practitioners* (John Wiley & Sons, 2015).

Barlow, D. H., *The Oxford Handbook of Clinical Psychology* (Oxford University Press, 2014).

Beinart, H., Kennedy, P., & Llewelyn, S., *Clinical Psychology in Practice* (John Wiley & Sons, 2009).

Bennett-Levy, J. E., Butler, G. E., Fennell, M. E., Hackman, A. E., Mueller, M. E., & Westbrook, D. E., *Oxford Guide to Behavioural Experiments in Cognitive Therapy* (Oxford University Press, 2004).

Bentall, R. P., *Madness Explained: Psychosis and Human Nature* (Penguin Books, 2003).

Butler, G. & Hope, T., *Managing Your Mind: The Mental Fitness Guide* (Oxford University Press, 2007).

Cabaniss, D. L., Cherry, S., Douglas, C. J., & Schwartz, A. R., *Psychodynamic Psychotherapy: A Clinical Manual* (John Wiley & Sons, 2011).

Carr, A., *The Handbook of Child and Adolescent Clinical Psychology: A Contextual Approach* (Routledge, 2015).

Castonguay, L. G., & Beutler, L. E., *Principles of Therapeutic Change that Work* (Oxford University Press, 2006).

Cooper, M., *Essential Research Findings in Counselling and Psychotherapy: The Facts Are Friendly* (Sage Publications, 2008).

Eells, T. D., *Handbook of Psychotherapy Case Formulation* (Guilford Press, 2011).

Emerson, E., *Clinical Psychology and People with Intellectual Disabilities* (John Wiley & Sons, 2012).

Fleming, I., & Steen, L., *Supervision and Clinical Psychology: Theory, Practice and Perspectives* (Routledge, 2013).

Friedberg, R. D., & McClure, J. M., *Clinical Practice of Cognitive Therapy with Children and Adolescents: The Nuts and Bolts* (Guilford Press, 2015).

Golding, L., & Gray, I., *Continuing Professional Development for Clinical Psychologists: A Practical Handbook* (John Wiley & Sons, 2008).

Greenberger, D., & Padesky, C. A., *Mind Over Mood: Change How You Feel by Changing the Way You Think* (Guilford Press, 1995).

Hall, J., Pilgrim, D., Turpin, G., & Marks, S., *Clinical Psychology in Britain: Historical Perspectives* (British Psychological Society, 2015).

Hayes, S. C., Strosahl, K. D., & Wilson, K. G., *Acceptance and Commitment Therapy: The Process and Practice of Mindful Change* (Guilford Press, 2011).

Hecker, J., & Thorpe, G., *Introduction to Clinical Psychology* (Routledge, 2015).

Hersen, M., & Sturmey, P., *Handbook of Evidence-Based Practice in Clinical Psychology, Adult Disorders* (John Wiley & Sons, 2012).

Johnson, L., & Dallos. R., *Formulation in Psychology and Psychotherapy* (Routledge, 2013).

Jung, C., *Modern Man in Search of His Soul* (Harcourt, 1933). The extract is taken from p. 39.

Knight, A., *How to Become a Clinical Psychologist: Getting a Foot in the Door* (Routledge, 2005).

Lange, G., & Davison, J., *Clinical Psychology in Singapore: An Asian Casebook* (NUS Press, 2015).

Llewelyn, S., & Murphy, D., *What is Clinical Psychology?* (Oxford University Press, 2014).

Malan, D., *Individual Psychotherapy and the Science of Psychodynamics* (Hodder Arnold, 2002).

Martin, P., & Birnbrauer, J. S., *Clinical Psychology: Profession and Practice in Australia* (Macmillan Education, 1996).

Miller, W. R., & Rollnick, S., *Motivational Interviewing: Helping People Change* (Guilford Press, 2012).

Morrison, A., Renton, J., Dunn, H., Williams, S., & Bentall, R., *Cognitive Therapy for Psychosis: A Formulation-Based Approach* (Routledge, 2004).

Roth, A., & Fonagy, P., *What Works for Whom? A Critical Review of Psychotherapy Research* (Guilford Press, 2013).

Ryan, F., *Cognitive Therapy for Addiction: Motivation and Change* (John Wiley & Sons, 2012).

Ryle, A., & Kerr, I. B., *Introducing Cognitive Analytic Therapy: Principles and Practice* (John Wiley & Sons, 2003).

Sacks, O., *The Man Who Mistook His Wife for a Hat: And Other Clinical Tales* (Picador, 1998).

Smail, D.J., *Illusion and Reality: The Meaning of Anxiety* (Karnac, 1993).

VandenBos, G. R., *APA Dictionary of Clinical Psychology* (American Psychological Association, 2013).

Weisz, J. R., & Kazdin, A. E., *Evidence-Based Psychotherapies for Children and Adolescents* (Guilford Press, 2010).

Westbrook, D., Kennerley, H., & Kirk, J., *An Introduction to Cognitive Behaviour Therapy: Skills and Applications* (Sage Publications, 2011).

West, J., & Spinks, P., *Clinical Psychology in Action: A Collection of Case Studies* (Butterworth-Heinemann, 2013).

Woods, R. T., & Clare, L., *Handbook of the Clinical Psychology of Ageing* (Wiley Online Library, 2008).

Yalom, I. D., & Elkin, G., *Every Day Gets a Little Closer: A Twice-Told Therapy* (Basic Books, 2014).

Young, J. E., Klosko, J. S., & Weishaar, M. E., *Schema Therapy: A Practitioner's Guide* (Guilford Press, 2003).

Williams, M., & Penman, D., *Mindfulness: A Practical Guide to Finding Peace in a Frantic World* (Piatkus, 2011).

Index